Night Skies of Aboriginal Australia

A Noctuary

Dianne Johnson

SYDNEY UNIVERSITY PRESS

Originally published in 1998 by Oceania Publications

This reprint edition published in 2014 by SYDNEY UNIVERSITY PRESS

© Sydney University Press 2014

Sydney University Press
Fisher Library F03
University of Sydney NSW 2006
AUSTRALIA
Email: sup.info@sydney.edu.au

National Library of Australia Cataloguing-in-Publication entry

Author: Johnson, Dianne D. (Dianne Dorothy), author.

Title: Night skies of Aboriginal Australia : a noctuary / Dianne Johnson.

Edition: Reprint edition.

ISBN: 9781743323878 (paperback)

Subjects: Astronomy, Aboriginal Australian.

            Aboriginal Australians--Folklore.

Dewey Number:

            520.994

Cover image

This 40 x 60cm painting is by Mick Namerari Tjapaltjarri, a Pintupi man born c.1925. Painted in 1978, it depicts the rising sun on the right hand side, with the daylight behind it, chasing away the black night on the left. The central circles are labelled a 'special place' and the white dots are painted stones, although they could also be seen as stars or campfires.

© The estate of the artist licensed by Aboriginal Artists Agency Ltd.

Contents

List of figures

Note to the 2014 Edition

Peter White

A noctuary is a record of what passes during the night, the opposite of diary, a daytime record. *Night Skies of Aboriginal Australia*, which includes material from the Torres Strait Islands, is not only this but, as its author anthropologist Diane Johnson says, an appreciation of Aboriginal stories and ideas. Since its publication in 1998, Oceania Monograph 47 has been in continuing demand, and this reprint will allow it to have a wider circulation. Apart from minor corrections, the original text and illustrations are unchanged. Readers who wish to explore the subject further should search the subject on the internet, since there have been a number of more recent specific studies by several authors.

Acknowledgements

The early stages of my research for this project were carried out when I was working in the Department of Anthropology under Emeritus Professor Michael Allen at the University of Sydney. I am grateful for the resources made available to me by that department. Just when my research efforts were nearing the end, Jim Smith of Wentworth Falls let me loose in his library and my research efforts began anew. Members of the Leura Adult Literature Discussion Group, always a receptive and supportive audience, alerted me to his knowledge and expertise. Paul Alexander quietly encouraged and extended the boundaries of my known anthropological universe. John Clegg and Jadran Mimica asked uncomfortable questions about assumptions I had made. Friedegard Tomasetti listened and supported ideas with library searches and articles. Sascha Zdenkowski and Hugh Speirs persevered with my technological idiocy. Robyn Wood typset the manuscript with her usual proficiency. And, as always, fellow stargazers Susan Wilson, Sophie and George Zdenkowski displayed unflagging confidence in this project and a persistent irritating optimism. For their generosity, I am grateful to them all.

'Who would deny the sacrilege of grasping
an unwilling heaven, enslaving it, as it were,
in its own domain, and fetching it to earth?'
(Manilius)

'It was the grandeur of a mechanistic
universe, awesome and awful, that banished
in its chilly light the last shadows of the
mythic universe, a universe in which
shivering human beings stood and reassured
one another of its glory and wonder'.
(Harrison)

Preface

With the 1986 apparition of Halley's Comet, I ventured out with a mild curiosity and discovered the night sky. Being in Australia, my night sky is the southern hemisphere, and, as I slowly learned the major southern sky constellations, I found myself becoming increasingly fascinated by the names and their associated stories. Star-hopping around the backdrop of the heavens, I traced out their patterns and, on the way, made up a few of my own! The fact that they'd been named from the perspective of northern hemisphere viewers many centuries before, escaped me for a while, until, belatedly, I found that I had mistakenly set quite a few of them the right way up. So, for example, the constellation of the lion, Leo, I made with paws down, head erect and his tail (to make sense of the stars in that area), I placed at the end of his body, but standing straight upward, as though he was permanently in a state of sheer terror. As this exercise was carried out in the privacy of my own head, I did not worry too much about small odd details such as this. That is, until it slowly dawned that all the so-named northern hemisphere constellations were drawn to make sense to northern hemisphere dwellers, with the result that many appear upside down to us southerners. The apparent arbitrary nature of the star groupings, those which the Ancients had designated 'belonged' together, began to interest me greatly. I took to wondering how other peoples had patterned their skies, in particular, the first Australians. Beyond the cities, Australian nightscapes are renowned for their brilliance and grandness, and it made sense that they must have played a significant role in the cultural life of Australian Aboriginal people. I subsequently combed the anthropological literature and read hundreds of myths. This then, is a composite of non-Aboriginal versions of Aboriginal astronomical ideas. It represents an attempt to rescue from esoteric texts, some of the rich and fabulous stories and ideas which constitute Aboriginal astronomy. It is an appreciation.

1

Prologue

The Children Learn
'Tis evening, the glistening sun sinks low,
The crested waves of Mulkeong[1] roll by.
The shadows of the trees creep out and grow,
While languidly the campfires' smoke curls high;
And sitting near a humpy on the beach,
Is Badjeru with children all in a row,
Chanting to them the ancient songs which teach
Them all those things that happened long ago ...
The sun goes down, the children's voices fall,
The shadows creep upon them and they hear
Out of the dark the curlew's warning call;
The spirits of the night are somewhere near.
The men around their fires burst into song.
The children's play is finished, while nearby
Upon the sandy beach of Mulkeong
Dark casuarinas bow with grace, and sigh.[2]

The nomadic lifestyle of the Australian Aborigines, camping out beneath the stars for thousands of years before the invention of the light globe and electricity, lent itself particularly well to star gazing. Sleeping and dreaming under clear, dark night skies near warming campfires was something the Aboriginal people could take for granted. Except for the full moon, the low glow of fires was the only illuminant at night. Even today, many non-urban Aboriginal people still prefer to sleep out, despite having houses. When rain falls, they are, of course, glad to have

---

1 Mulkeong: a camp site near Cape Barrow, Gulf of Carpentaria.

2 Harney and Elkin 1949:65–66.

a roof, but most of the year they still prefer to sleep in their swags out on the ground next to fires, tucked up with blankets, their ceiling the night sky.

Australian Aboriginal and Torres Strait Islander people before white contact, explored and embraced darkness: they experienced its many and varied dimensions and were contained by it. The rhythm of the night, as much as the day or the season, dictated activity and gave meaning to everyday life. There is every reason to think that they had developed in their myriad languages, words and concepts to describe the onset of darkness for example, its gradations of colour and varieties in tone, as well as phenomena of luminosity, a vocabulary which described and gave meaning to the darkness and the night.

Before the widespread use of the light globe, Western cultures experienced a different relationship with darkness, one which involved less alienation and a greater familiarity. Aspects of language reflected this familiarity with things nocturnal. Consider the range of words and concepts now fallen into desuetude. In times yore, as evening darkled, noctivagant and noctambulous folk sought noctilucence; darkmans, although sometimes filled with wickedness was confronted in noctuaries. Darkling, noctivagators happened upon night-hacks, -hawks and -hunters.[3]

One of the most significant characteristics of urbanised Australia is the organisation of daily life around light, be it fuelled by the sun or the light globe. Night in urban Australia is an experience of darkness mediated. Not even the night sky is particularly dark: even in fine and moonless weather, it is cloaked in a pink and pudgy veil. And when the house lights are switched off or turned low, most turn to their beds to re-assure containment from the darkness.

---

3 Translated: In past times, as the evening became dark, those folk who roamed and wandered in the night sought things that shone through the darkness: night, though sometimes perceived as sinister was confronted in accounts about what happened on a particular night or nights. In the dark, those who wandered in the night, came upon night-watchmen or policemen, thieves and burglars who specialised in night work, as well as poachers and prostitutes.

The modern city-dweller's experience of darkness, of the night, is relatively limited in everyday life, since the city at night is a place delineated by patterns of lights: from dazzling neon flashes to ashen spaces. The joyless connecting passages, the shadow-alleys, sombre stairwells and murky basements, are assiduously avoided and cast as ominous places, filled with potential danger and violence. Evil. Threatening. Darkness is not perceived as being safe to explore. It is best avoided.

There are, of course, night people in the city. But with the exclusion of some garbage collecters, street sweepers, fishermen, tramps and vagrants, they undertake their activities in illuminated, indoor places and spaces, be they hospital, factory or hospitality workers, security agents, cleaners, taxi-drivers, or all-night party-goers. When city dwellers do venture out beyond the lights of the city into the darkness, it is usually in organised packs – groups or clubs – for night prowls, for star gazing parties or for evening barbeques. Fear and loathing of the dark is mitigated by the gathering of the herd.

Australian Aboriginal and Torres Strait Islander people, although at times fearful of the dark and its creatures, did not seek to avoid it. The night was but another landscape. As the American astronomer Chet Raymo muses:

Perhaps it is only in the dark that the eye and the mind, turning to each other, can cooperate in the delicate and impassioned art of seeing. Few people willingly choose to walk the dark path, to enter the knot of fear in the stomach, or to live in the black cave of the sleepless night. But then, unexpectedly, the ... truth emerges. The light of the mind returns bearing extraordinary gifts.[4]

Much of this particular discussion about Australian Aboriginal and Torres Strait Islander astronomical concepts, classifications and mythologies is based on observations and accounts collected and written many decades ago. The fragmentary nature of these accounts is spread randomly through reports, articles, journals and stories making a coherent and comprehensive assessment difficult; nevertheless, they provide tantalising glimpses. The majority of ethnographers, ethnologists, surveyors and observers of Aboriginal cultural practices after

4 Raymo 1985:20.

white invasion and settlement were severely limited in most cases, by their lack of knowledge about astronomy within their own cultural traditions. For the most part, they were unable to engage with Aboriginal people in any detail or depth about Aboriginal astronomical concepts and classifications. Some sort of mutually understood reference system is necessary for the information to be exchanged and recorded and many early ethnologists found themselves unable to identify the celestial phenomena discussed by their Aboriginal informants, as indicated for example by Maegraith[5] in Central Australia. Charles Mountford also notes:

> Although in the early days among the Aborigines my wonder at, as well as my pleasure in, the stars had been great, they were backed by little information. True I could recognise Orion, Scorpio and, of course, the Southern Cross, but the constellations of Argo, Delphinus, Hercules and many others were beyond me.[6]

Fortunately, Mountford's star knowledge increased greatly and is demonstrated in his later work.[7]

In addition, many of the early observers did not have the expertise to unravel cultural interconnections associated with astronomy. Aboriginal astronomical knowledge was not discrete and separate from other aspects of cultural life. It was interwoven into song, dance, ritual, art and myth, and certain aspects could be owned by one group of people to the complete or partial exclusion of another. Time constraints also limited the extent of detail observed and discussed, as noted by, for example, the surveyor Mathews.[8] The observers were frequently employed doing other work and their recording of Aboriginal cultural practices were undertaken after their other work was concluded for the day. The specific locations within Australia that I have identified in this

---

5 Maegraith 1932:24.

6 1948:164.

7 Mountford 1956: 1976b.

8 Mathews 1905.

discussion represent the locales of activity by early ethnologists as much as particular sites of Aboriginal astronomical beliefs. These beliefs and astronomical observations were clearly spread the length and breadth of the country. Most went undocumented.

The very few articles that have been written, which in any way directly address Aboriginal astronomy, show a tendency to look for pictures or geometric grid-map equivalents of Western constellation patterns, as in Isaacs (1980), Bhathal and White (1991) and Haynes (1992). Stars in Aboriginal culture are, rather, read as a series of multi-dimensional, inter-connected cognitive maps or aesthetic expressions based on a distinctive, separate and integrated cosmology.

Increasingly in recent years, anthropologists, sociologists and historians have concerned themselves with identifying the specific links between natural knowledge and the social, intellectual and aesthetic contexts in which it is produced. Differing social orders produce differing accounts of natural reality.

Anthropologists have long been concerned with understanding the multivarious conceptions of nature in preliterate societies. Needless to say, these conceptions show wide and fundamental divergences from those that characterise the modern 'scientific' conceptions of Western societies. Moreover, one conception cannot elucidate the other: western astronomical classifications and concepts will not elucidate Aboriginal ones. At risk of stating the obvious, Australian Aboriginal ideas about stars and their place in the cosmos were a product of Aboriginal culture.

One of the controversies in social anthropology has been concerned with identifying precisely how such cosmologies should be understood. Are preliterate conceptions of nature analagous to modern science as envisaged by the rather Eurocentric anthropologists such as Frazer and Tylor of the ninteenth century? Clearly, equating preliterate conceptions of nature with modern science renders these conceptions as inferior, inadequate science, one that is informed by less rational ideas than those of Western science. If, on the other hand, they are viewed as responses to social interests, they can then be understood as rational and adequate responses.[9]

---

9 See Barnes 1973.

Horton's contribution to this debate has been useful. While he considers preliterate cosmologies to be attempts to understand and explain nature as are scientific theories, the models used by preliterate societies for structuring their ideas about nature are based on their perceived organisation of their own societies. How the society is organised becomes the model for how nature is organised. Explanations of the unfamiliar in terms of the familiar are universal and natural modes of thought.[10] For Horton, the social order is a resource available to be used like any other in the rational construction of a cognitive system about natural order. Certainly, the Australian Aboriginal people used their kinship and marriage system to explain the intricacies of relations between stars, but the question posed by Douglas[11] nags: why use this particular model over all others?

Douglas argues that people choose to use a particular model so that the particular model is reinforced, justified and legitimated. Natural orders are not necessarily akin to social orders.[12] Thus, when a model of kinship and marriage is projected onto the night sky by, for example, the Aranda people of Central Australia[13], as well as describing and explaining an aspect of their cosmos, they are actively trying to maintain an institution that has served them well.

Other anthropological writings[14] argue for the employment of different analogies: rather than science, it is to art or theatre in Western cultural traditions that we should turn in order to understand the preliterate cosmos. Beattie[15] goes so far as to suggest that there is a basic and absolute divide between the interests which inform art and magical belief on the one hand, and science and technology on the other. Modern science, in his view, has completely rid itself of any expressive

---

10 Horton 1971:223–25.
11 Douglas 1975.
12 Douglas 1966:90–92.
13 Maegraith 1932.
14 For example Firth:1932.
15 Beattie 1966:63–5.

or symbolic interest. Preliterate representations of nature, then, like art, have little interest in simply depicting or communicating reliable information as a secure basis for practical action: they are of another realm, their concern being to symbolise aspects of society and give aesthetic satisfaction and value.

As indicated by Shapin,[16] not one of these viewpoints considers the specific context within which preliterate cosmologies are revealed. In other words, what were the specific contexts in Aboriginal societies in which discussions about the cosmos arose, its motifs were drawn and its knowledge passed on? Unfortunately, not a lot is known. There are, however, hints concerning the passage of Aboriginal star knowledge from one person to another and from one generation to the next.

Myths concerning stars and other celestial phenomena, as with all myths, were divided and passed on in accordance with their ownership by specific men and women. There were myths belonging to men with male heroes as the central characters and enacted in ceremonies by men alone, and there were myths belonging to women with emphasis on female characters and enacted by women alone. There were also myths belonging to men that were dramatised with women playing minor parts under the authority of men. In some contexts, women and children were permitted to see parts of these ritual enactments, but for long periods, they had to lie face downwards with their eyes hidden, while the men patrolled to ensure there was no peeking. As well, there were myths belonging primarily to men but also shared by women and, in dramatisations of these, both female and male characters were emphasised and the enactments of male and female were undertaken by each gender respectively.[17]

Observations in South Australia by the anthropologist Isobel White lead her to assert that older, ritually significant men and women knew at least some of the secret myths of the other. For example, the Yalata stories of the Seven Sisters cycle of myths, from the star cluster known in Western culture as the Pleiades, belong primarily in that part of the

16 Shapin 1979:49.
17 White 1975:125.

country to the men of the group, but both female and male characters were emphasised, with men enacting their particular dramas within it and women separately enacting theirs. Yet among the Wolmeri of the Kimberley region, a myth concerned with the moon was associated with ritual and ceremonial activity only witnessed by men.[18]

There is no doubt that in Aboriginal culture astronomical knowledge was considered to be extremely important, so much so that it was described as being one of the 'principal branches of education'.[19] Among groups between the rivers Leigh and Glenelg in western Victoria, for example, star knowledge was taught by men particularly known for their intelligence and expertise.[20] Particular families, too, had a reputation for possessing more exact astronomical knowledge than others.[21]

Many of the narratives associated with the night sky were for general consumption. The surveyor Mathews, who visited many Aboriginal groups in New South Wales and Victoria, observed:

> Throughout the summer months, and during fine weather at other periods, the blacks usually camp out in the open air, where they have every opportunity of watching the starry vault above them. The face of the moon, who was a human being in ancient times, wending its way through these stars month after month, helps to increase the people's interest. There are always some clever old men in the camp, who are the recognised repositories of the lore of the tribe, who take advantage of this outdoor life to teach the young people stories about some of the different stars which may be visible at such times. As soon as an old man commences one of these stories, the young folk from the neighbouring campfires con-

18 Kaberry 1939:12.

19 Dawson 1981:99.

20 However, star knowledge was not held exclusively by males in this region as Dawson was taught by Weerat Kuyuut a sagacious elder of the Moporr group as well as his intelligent daughter Yarrum Parpur Tarneen and her husband, Wombeet Tuulawarn.

21 Stanbridge (1857) in Smythe (1972:432) reports that he knew one such family from the Boorong group in the Mallee area of Victoria.

gregate around him and listen avidly to his marvellous narra-
tions ... the young people of the audience listen so attentively
that they are themselves able, in years long after, to repeat
the stories to another generation. In this way the star myths
and other native legends have been handed down from time
immemorial.[22]

Bill Neidjie, an elder of the Gagadju people in the Northern Territory
explains:

My grandpa taught me that [star and seasonal knowledge].

He said, 'Don't forget this.

tell this story with kids ...

so he can listen

slow,

and then the story will come for him ...

exactly like this.

This story right, exactly right,

because it dreaming.'

We all lying down on grass in dry season.

Look up at stars,

I tell kids,

'See them stars ...

they been there million years

they always be there.[23]

Particular star knowledge was associated specifically with male initiation and the process of gradual attainment of wisdom. In Central
Australia, for example, astronomical knowledge was handed down by
older men to the boys at the time of their initiation, and it was carefully
concealed from the women. As a result, the women, according to one
observer[24], knew 'practically nothing about the stars.'[25] Another report

---

22 Mathews 1905:76.

23 Neidjie 1985:55–56.

24 Maegraith 1932:5.

25 The credibility of this statement is somewhat dubious as Maegraith (a
male) only used male informants.

suggests that all the adult men of the western Central Desert were 'fully conversant with the star lore of their tribe, (whereas) the young men appear(ed) to be almost ignorant of any astronomical knowledge until they (had) passed through their initiation rituals.'[26] Further south in the Ooldea region of South Australia, this also was the case: 'Most of the totemic ancestral beings (were) represented in the sky by stars and planets ... knowledge of the stars ... properly belong(ed) to the secret life of the men.'[27] Daisy Bates suggests that this is also true among the Bibbulmun in Western Australia[28], as it was among the lower River Murray group, the Jaralde in South Australia.[29] Of course, the content and timing of these ritual activities varied dramatically across the continent.

The Australian land mass constitutes a vast area, straddling some 33 degrees of latitude—from 43° S in Tasmania to 10° S in the Torres Strait. Not only was there a great range in the actual night skies seen at any one time across Australia, there was, as well, a variety in the environments from which they were seen. It is therefore not possible to talk of one, over-arching 'Aboriginal astronomy'. Recent articles[30] about stars in Aboriginal culture have assumed such a notion. However, it is a notion that blurs place, time, space, language and cultural differences between and within groups of people who have inhabited the Australian continent and its islands for over 60,000 years before European invasion and settlement. Aboriginal people had some 600 languages and dialects,

---

26 Mountford (1976b:89) also asserts that women were not aware of the secret myths about the night sky, but adds that the women had their own separate secret stories and myths about the heavenly bodies.

27 Lewis (1942–45:64) relying on the fieldwork of the Berndts in the Ooldea region.

28 Bates 1992:170.

29 Berndt and Berndt (1993:66–37) report that knowledge about the stars, about moon phases and the tides was passed from older men to boys during initiation in the form of myths as the stories of the ancestral heroes, many represented as stars, were interwoven into and causally related to seasonal and ritual activities.

30 Bhathal and White (1991) and Haynes (1992).

had distinct cultural practices and lived in wide-ranging and dynamic ecological contexts: from hunter/gatherer coastal, riverine, through grassland, forest and desert environments to more sedentary cultivation in the Torres Strait Islands. So the landscapes from which the cosmos was viewed, the spirit of place, varied considerably. In addition, constellations and celestial phenomena seen in the south were never seen in the more northerly climes of the country and vice versa, thus, the variations in night skies themselves were dissimilar.

It is clear that the particular contexts in which knowledge about the stars was produced differed from locality to locality; different bodies of knowledge, in detail at least, arose in different contexts. So that the ways in which the stars were grouped and classified also varied across the country, lending further support for the view that classifications of the natural world are 'made' or invented rather than 'found' or discovered. They are thus sustained and modified in response to changing patterns of social contingencies, each constantly verified according to its own particular terms of reference.[31]

One branch of social anthropology in particular, that of cognitive anthropology, took up aspects of this inquiry with great enthusiasm. It focussed on discovering how different peoples organise and use their cultural frameworks, attempting in the process to understand the organising principles underlying behaviour. In this tradition, cultures are not viewed as material phenomena, but rather as cognitive organisations of material phenomena.[32] Furthermore, not only may phenomena be organised differently from one culture to another, but they may be organised in more than one way within the same culture. There is intracultural as well as intercultural variation. The transformations may result from either different classes of people or different situations and contexts.[33] As a consequence of this interest in variation comes the notion that cultures and cultural phenomena cannot be described or

---

31 Dean (1979:213) in Barnes and Shapin.

32 Tyler 1969:.

33 Goodenough 1957:57–64.

explained by only one set of organising principles. So it is, that only some people may have expert knowledge about stars in Aboriginal societies and certain alternatives are emphasised to explain or describe particular contexts.

The night sky was viewed by Aboriginal and Torres Strait Islander peoples as being multi-layered. Its meanings operate at many levels simultaneously and vary with the particular filter which is overlaid. When, for example, the night sky is viewed as a seasonal calendar, it does not exclude meanings it has in mythologies or social relationships, as these aspects frequently elaborate the seasonal manifestations. It represents a shift in emphasis. Stars used for seasonal voyaging do not exclude at the same time, their meaning in a terrestrial landscape. Moreover, knowing them as belonging to the place of the dead, for example, does not preclude seeing them as patterns of living celestial campfires. The Aboriginal sky then was a series of inter-connected multi-layered maps. These maps are in complementary distribution and do not conflict with one another.[34] They create order, and from this order, prediction is theoretically possible.

Putting order and meaning into the night sky has long fired the imagination of human beings. The 4000 or so naked-eye bright objects, let alone the sprays of illumination and the innumerable bounded dark spaces, can present as utter chaos. There is no intrinsic reason why the points of light, the luminous sprays and the dark patches cannot be organised into two-dimensional geometric shapes—squares, triangles, circle— or indeed into three-dimensional shapes—cubes, cylinders, cones and prisms. Or into parallel lines, or even diagonals. Outlines of foods maybe—hamburgers, pizzas and the like. Why not bush tucker or hunting implements? Why not campfires of the dead or the tracks of ancestral spirits?

We classify because life in a world of sameness would be intolerable. Yet inordinate diversity could be extremely daunting. By naming and classifying, the rich world of infinite variability shrinks to manipulative

---

34 Tyler 1969:5.

size and becomes bearable, understandable and ultimately meaningful. Naming is one of the chief methods of imposing order on what is perceived, the names showing both what is significant in an environment as well as how the perceptions of that environment are organised and ordered.[35] Ultimately, the ways in which we classify are arbitrary.

In the chapters following, the order and its subsequent meanings imposed by the Aboriginal people on their night sky shall unfold. I begin with a global view of Aboriginal cosmological concepts, moving on to accounts of the day-to-day uses of this knowledge, discussing inscription of knowledge in speech, on persons and on the body. Finally I frame the account 'scientifically' and then historically.

In chapter 2, I shall elucidate how Aboriginal people viewed their cosmos and the hand they had in its continuity. The sky-dome and the sky-world beyond were part of everyday life for Aboriginal people: their cosmos was vibrant and animated, teeming with interactive energies.

The focus moves to the 'practical' uses to which star knowledge was put by Aboriginal people. Having imposed order on the cosmos, Aboriginal people used stars for predictive purposes in their hunting and gathering economies (and in cultivation in the case of the Torres Strait Islanders). Ritual activity was a highly significant cultural adjunct to their economic life and timing was crucial to its efficacy. Navigation, both terrestrial and marine, is also considered.

Oral accounts of the sky, including references in mythology, are explored in the next chapter. Social relations and kin ties that are projected onto the heavens are the focus of chapter 5, and, from concern with persons, I move to a brief account of the stars and healing of the body. Aboriginal notions as they relate to European astronomy are investigated in Chapter 6 and the change in cosmological views following White invasion informs the final chapter.

---

35 Anthropological accounts of taxonomies have abounded and include Subanum terminology of skin diseases (Frake 1961), colour categorisation (Berlin and Kay 1971; Conklin 1955), kinship terminologies (Lounsbury 1964), zoological classifications (Diamond 1966; Bulmer 1967) and plant classification (Berlin, Breedlove and Raven 1973).

As the sources of information are widely scattered and come with differing levels of interest and expertise, there is no continuity in the use of terms to describe traditional social and territorial organisations, an area in anthropological discourse which is beset with controversy. In general, I have deliberately refrained from using such terms (except where they appear in quotations) such as - tribe, language unit, domain, range, estate, band, culture-area, drainage division, phratry, clan - not out of a desire to avoid clear manifestations of political process among Aboriginal people, but rather as a way of rendering the material more accessible. I have, however, attempted to preserve the persistence of association, so strongly asserted by Aboriginal people, between people and place.

The majority of the material collected about Australian Aboriginal astronomy relies on observations and accounts from the nineteenth and early twentieth centuries. The bulk of these observations is derived from men (and a few women) who carried with them their own cultural perceptions and experiences about what constituted for example, 'astronomy', 'sky' and in turn, 'night sky'. There is no word or concept in the many Aboriginal languages for the Western concept 'astronomy' or indeed 'astrology'. There was no separate domain of inquiry or knowledge, in as much as the night sky was not a separate space from other aspects of the landscape.

The early observers of Aboriginal and Torres Strait Islander life came from a post-Newtonian Europe in which the safe, mechanistic, self-running, self-sustaining, perfectly ordered universe of the eighteenth century had been replaced by a universe which, having pushed humans off centre stage, was challenging deeply held and cherished notions about order, hierarchy and consequently, meaning. The cosmologist, Edward Harrison explains that 'it is hopeless trying to understand the nineteenth century, with its fulminations from pulpit to platform, without realizing that numerous persons were struggling to save the imperiled world pictures that gave meaning and purpose to life on Earth.'[36]

---

36 Harrison 1985: 110.

In collecting impressions about Aboriginal and Torres Strait Islander cosmologies and astronomies, the early observers did not ask questions about how 'sky' was experienced, construed or constructed. Such problematic notions as what is perceived by Aboriginal people as properly belonging to the linguistic category 'sky' and how celestial phenomena were perceived in this context are not addressed. Whether 'sky' had distance, time or boundary, or indeed, what constituted these categories, were not considerations at that time. Problems of nomenclature add to the complexity. In simple terms, modern Western astronomy has constructed an imagined Euclidean geometric grid over the night sky and patterns of the constellations are determined by joining dot-to-faint-dot, points of lights. The resulting dark spaces and light patterns are then ordered and named through a combination of Greek, Arabic and European naming and numeral systems. Australian Aboriginal and Torres Strait Islander skies do not lend themselves to such geometrical interpretations. Importantly, Harrison has noted that 'within one's own universe it is extremely difficult to reconstruct a universe of long ago. The historical method recreates the past as perceived and understood within the cosmic framework of the historian.[37]

The taxonomic dilemmas thrown up by the data are seemingly infinite! What delineates 'night', for example: how is darkness perceived and experienced? Are there gradations, qualities and textures present in Aboriginal ideas about 'darkness'? Western astronomy draws very clear distinctions between celestial veils and flashes of luminescence: comets for example, are distinguished from meteorites. How these celestial movements, their direction, luminosity and remnants were perceived by Aboriginal people is again problematic. Are what Europeans perceive as craters in the landscape related to meteor impacts? Does what we call 'weather' and discuss ad infinitum, have an equivalent? Is it related to, or located in 'sky'? Indeed, what is 'sky'? Does it have boundaries, texture or distance? Are heat and light necessarily associated with that dominating celestial object we know as 'sun'? Does it have an identity? Does

---

37 Harrison 1985:1.

it really watch us interminably, with its huge monster eye? What holds the moon up there? Why doesn't it fall down? Why does the sunset rise and set to a myriad of colours? The problems inherent in really comprehending each others' universes are, to say the least, formidable!

It does seem clear, however, that at least some star knowledge and mythology was deemed secret and sacred. Consequently, this knowledge is not available; it was, and still is where possible, guarded by Aboriginal people, kept from those whom they see to be involved in appropriation or devaluation, or simply from those who are not initiated into Aboriginal cultural life or who are not of Aboriginal descent. Chet Raymo, astronomer-academic, having visited Central Australia to see the 1985/86 visitation of Halley's Comet, judged this to be a reasonable stance:

> The Aborigines who live near Ayers Rock are reluctant to share the secrets of the monolith with non-Aboriginal Australians or even uninitiated Aborigines. They firmly believe that knowledge of the Dreamtime must be judiciously communicated if the health of the cosmos is to be preserved. There is, I think, wisdom in the Aboriginal reticence. I am a teacher and a writer. It is my business to communicate the Dreamtime stories of science to as wide an audience as possible. But I am reluctant to allow scientific knowledge to be depreciated by becoming trivial and commonplace. When we sell comets the way we sell tooth-paste, something essential has been lost in our quest to understand nature ... Astronomy, after all, is a science of faint lights. The excitement of astronomy lies in the way grand knowledge has been distilled from blurs of light in the night sky. One blur is a nebula where stars are born from streamers of dust and gas. Another is the debris of a stellar explosion, fat with heavy elements for future planets. Other blurs are clusters, quasars, galaxies racing outward from the impulse of the Big Bang or comets bearing hints of the origin of life. These faint lights, creatively interpreted, have conveyed to us the secrets of our Dreamtime.[38]

38 Raymo 1986:11.

2

Aboriginal Cosmology

Australian Aboriginal cosmology, as with all cosmologies, changed and refined itself as Aboriginal people themselves changed and recast themselves. Their view of their world or universe by the time of White contact had developed, modified and transformed itself over many thousands of years, and any attempts to reconstruct or recover a single version of their cosmology from the frozen frame of early anthropological accounts is, to say the least, challenging. Nevertheless, it is the case that their conceptions of their universe(s) were constructed by them and reflected their particular social, economic, political and aesthetic concerns at any particular time. Like us, they were involved in an ongoing formulation and reformulation of their cosmos. According to Harrison,

> The universes are our models of the Universe. They are the great schemes of intricate thought—grand cosmic pictures— that rationalise human experience; these universes harmonise and invest with meaning the rising and setting Sun, the waxing and waning Moon, the jewelled lights of the night sky, the landscape of rocks and trees and clouds. Each universe is a self-consistent system of ideas, marvellously organised, interlacing most of what is perceived and known ... Wherever we find a human society, however primitive, there is a universe, and wherever we find a universe, of whatever kind, there is a society; both go together, and the one does not exist without the other. Each universe coordinates and unifies a society, enabling its members to communicate their thoughts and share their experiences. Each universe determines what is perceived and what constitutes valid knowledge, and the members of each society believe what is perceived and perceive what is believed.[1]

---

1 Harrison 1985:2.

There are a few basic tenets that underpin a general understanding of Aboriginal cosmology. In Aboriginal ideas about the universe, nature and society, with all its cultural accoutrements, were formed at the same time by powerful creative spirits who wandered the earth during an eternal time (still existing), known these days simply as 'The Dreaming'.[2] These ancestral spirits still abound but are usually no longer visible, having withdrawn from human view into another space/time realm. The earth and life itself were seen as having been in existence when the great creative powers began their business. However, these spirits are not seen as being omnipotent, in the sense that humans, too, are considered to be co-creators. Their task is to maintain the ecological balance, being ultimately responsible for the ongoing harmony between natural and cultural systems, harmony and balance being seen as the keys to the health and continuity of the two systems. '(Aboriginal) human beings have a responsibility to intervene where they consider intervention necessary and to leave things alone when they consider that necessary. Humans have the ability to adjust the system, as well as throw it out of kilter'.[3]

The sustaining effects are seen as theoretically reciprocal: if people work to support natural systems, attending as stewards to the continuity of various species, natural plenty is assured for the continuity of people and their cultural practices. Aboriginal ritual life (increase, initiatory and mourning rites) are thus concerned, at the level of ideology at least, with assurance of the continuity of life - the natural increase of species (increase or fertility rites), the social existence of persons (initiatory rites) and the ongoing nature of the spirit (mourning rites). These rituals 'seize upon traditions which may be naturally occurring, as with the flowering of trees from which nectar is obtained, or socially occurring, as with the making of men from boys ... Life is seen ... as cyclical, as running a course, and it is the responsibility of ritual performers to keep natural and social cycles in motion'.[4]

---

2 See Stanner 1991.

3 Rose 1992:97.

4 Maddock 1974:132.

Aboriginal cosmology then, is more than a creation theory about the origin and structure of the world; it involves as well a theory of human participation and action.

The Sky Dome

Despite my cautionary notes about different cosmologies, it is occasionally possible to identify universal themes. Most Australian Aboriginal people held a common view of the earth as a flat disc surrounded by the boundless water of an ocean. Above this earth-disc was a solid vault or canopy. Beyond this vault was the sky-world, a vast, plentiful and beautiful place. 'The sky was a canopy covering all and coming down beyond the horizon to meet and enclose the flat surface on which men and women followed the fixed pattern of their lives'.[5]

The sky dome or canopy was usually supported by props of one sort or another. Views about what constituted the props differed across the country. In the Australian Alps for example, the vault was held up by trees[6], but on the New South Wales coast, the props appear also to have been solid wooden pillars watched over and guarded by an old man.[7] In some places, the stars seen as star-people held the canopy up in conjunction with an emu whose camp was in the dark patch near the

---

5 Willey 1979:51. The sky viewed as a vault above the disc-earth is well documented in the anthropological literature. It is a view held by Victorian groups (Mathews 1905:6; Massola 1968:05), in particular in western and central Victoria (Worms 1986:09); among New South Wales groups in general (Mathews 1905:6) and amongst the Wuradjeri of western New South Wales in particular (Berndt 1946–7:60); among the Yarralin people of the Victoria River Valley in the Northern Territory (Rose 1992:4); the Anyamatana people of the Northern Flinders in South Australia (Mountford 1939:103) and the Karadjeri of north Western Australia (Piddington 1932:94)

6 Worms 1986:109.

7 Willey 1979:34.

Southern Cross known to Europeans as the Coal Sack.[8] Myths told to Daisy Bates by people from the Great Australian Bight indicate that the sky-dome was held up by a great tree, known as *Warda*, which had to be protected at all times,[9] an idea similarly held by groups in the east.

The vault itself was pictured as being composed of a very hard and durable substance. The Karadjeri of north Western Australia, for example, thought this substance to be rock or shell.[10] Likewise, groups in Central Australia saw the dome as being 'a huge shell that covers the world during the hours of darkness ... the whole sky is turned over by the two men, the older and younger guardians of the circumcision ceremony ... who live in the constellation of Scorpius'.[11] The vault delineated the edge of the sky-world which was thought to be the dwelling place of many ancestral spirits and heroes, who were also personified sources of energy which informed and gave meaning to natural and cultural life. The sky-world could be visited by men and women of high degree (traditional healers) and their great powers were seen to be connected to these energies. Whether the vault was experienced as being consistently or uniformly contained, bounded or immutable is unclear.

Gaining Access to the Sky-World

The sky-world beyond the dome was envisaged as containing a hole, a window or a fissure, through which the traditional healers could gain entry. They usually gained access by climbing or pulling themselves up a connecting cord. The cord was seen variously as being hair, string, a rainbow, lightning, a spear, a grass rope, a tree, flames, a totem board and a turtle.[12] Among some Victorian groups there was a view that

8 Mountford 1976:27–31.

9 Isaacs 1980:141.

10 Piddington 1932:394.

11 Mountford 1976b:450.

12 Amongst the Dieri of Lake Eyre, it was a hair-cord (Elkin 1948:1), in the Northern Kimberleys, it was a rainbow (Elkin 1945:3) as it was

people used to be able to climb up an immense pine tree (probably *callitris* sp.), up through its branches to the topmost ones which reached the sky. They could walk about, indeed live on the starry vault. Those people who belonged to the sky could descend to the earth and likewise visit friends before returning. Visits were made for purposes of barter between hunting grounds. The tree was viewed as 'a regular highway between earth and the upper regions'.[13] Around the Roper River area, amongst the Alawa people in the Northern Territory, the link was also a tree, but more specifically, a large stringy-bark.[14] In an account of the Booandik people of South Australia, the healer (*pangal*) climbed to the sky-world quite regularly to visit and have social discourse with the sky people.[15]

In essence, the notion of a cord or link, an umbilicus, should be recognised as part of a myth cycle involving the life-giving or life-sustaining, connecting the earth and the present with the world above, the

---

amongst the Wik-Munkan people of Cape York Peninsula (McConnel 1957:115). In the Eastern Kimberleys, it was a string (Elkin 1945:3), amongst the Wotjobaluk in western New South Wales (Howitt 1904:04) and some Victorian groups (Mathews 1905:0), it was a pine tree (probably *callitris* sp.). Among the Wuradjeri of western New South Wales, it was a thread (Elkin 1945:5), amongst the Yarralin, lightning strings (Rose 1992:4–5), and at Menindee in New South Wales, and around Lake Alexandrina in South Australia, it was a spear (Berndt and Berndt 1977:03; 1993:29) as it was around Encounter Bay in South Australia (Meyer 1916:62). Amongst the Ngulugwongga people around Daly River in the Northern Territory, the Milky Way which was seen as a rope plaited from grass formed the link (Berndt and Berndt 1989:43–345). Around the Clarence River in New South Wales, it was seen to be the flames of a large fire (Mathews 1889:29). Among groups around the Great Australian Bight, it was a huge totem board, a symbolically decorated sheet of bark (Ker Wilson 1977:1–28), and among the Gundungurra in south-eastern New South Wales, it was a giant turtle (Smith 1992:4).

13 Mathews 1905:79–80.

14 Berndt and Berndt 1989:284.

15 Smith 1880:30.

eternal.[16] It was also possible in some areas to gain access to the sky-world by tunnelling through the earth to the other side of the sea.[17]

A myth explaining the sky-dome structure is told by the Mandalbingu people of northern Arnhem Land.[18] They tell the story of the first sunrise: how long, long ago, the sky was so close to the earth, it shut out all light. Everyone had to crawl around in darkness until the magpies, regarded as one of the more intelligent species of birds, decided that by working together, they could raise the sky. Slowly, using long sticks, they propped it on low boulders, then gradually onto higher boulders above their camp. As they struggled to lift the sky even higher, it suddenly split open to reveal the first sunrise. The beauty, light and warmth delighted the magpies, who burst into their distinctive warble. As they sang, the blanket of darkness broke into fragments and drifted away as clouds. Magpies, it is said, still greet the sunrise with their call.

Another myth from the headwaters of the Murrumbidgee River reiterates this same idea. The people from this region also envisaged the sky as once being very close to the earth, forcing people, plants, birds and animals to crawl. One day, the wife of an important elder ran off with another man. The elder took off after them. The couple took refuge in the waters of the river. In his search for them, the elder found a bright golden rod which when held up grew, pushing the sky upwards. Birds originally loathe to leave their cramped sky also went up. The elder is still somewhere pushing up the sky, and when he gets tired he lets the rod down. Whenever this happens, clouds cover the earth and fogs spread over the ground.[19]

---

16 Worms 1986:104.

17 This was a notion held for example, by the Wuradjeri (Berndt 1946–7:337).

18 Retold by Mountford (Roberts and Mountford 1974:98) and Gulpilil (Rule and Goodman 1979:15–23).

19 Peck 1925:30–37.

The people from the Great Australian Bight in South Australia see things a little differently. In one of their myths told to Daisy Bates[20] men and women of the Dreamtime (Dhoogoorr) lived forever. When they grew tired of being on earth, they simply walked back along the huge totem board (Kalligooroo), which joined the earth to Kalbu, the sky-country. They could return to earth whenever they wanted. There was also a third country (Jimbin) which lay beneath the earth. The spirit babies not yet born lived in this country but could only be born on earth. After birth and after their first smile, these spirit children became human children and could also travel with their mothers back and forth to the sky country. As the story goes, this totem board track was destroyed by a group of children who allowed their cooking fire to get out of control when they camped half-way along it.

So now, those who have gone to Kalbu, the sky-country, must remain there forever and those on earth cannot join Kalbu comrades again. Death, it is said, came to humans for the first time.

In other places as well as in the Great Australian Bight, there was a notion of an underworld which could be accessed by digging through the limited thickness of the earth. Amongst the Tiwi of Bathurst and Melville Islands in the Northern Territory, for example, the underworld was a place of complete darkness and contained a valley rimmed by two high stony ridges. Along the valley, the Sun Woman, guided by the light of a glowing bark torch, travelled each night from the western to the eastern horizon. Nothing grew in the underworld. The Sun Woman's act of lighting the fire of the bark torch was the first light of dawn and the clouds of sunrise were reddened by the dust of the powdered ochre she wore to decorate herself. The Moon Man also travellled along in the underworld valley by day and at night gave light to the stars above the earth.[21]

---

20 Ker Wilson 1977:21–22.

21 Sims 1978:166.

The Sky-World

Beyond the sky-dome or canopy is the sky-world. It is a dynamic and lively place, if somewhat mysterious. The sky-world of the Yarralin people of the Northern Territory, for example, is conceived as being above the stars but below the sun and the moon. It is the home of the Lightning People. When lightning is seen in the sky, it is known that the Lightning People are active, probably fighting. This sky-world is also the world of the dead, but after some time the spirit of a deceased person merges to become part of the collective Lightning People. A former healer from this area has described how he was taken to the sky-country for a fortnight when he was young. He described the place as peopled by men, women and children: 'The women had long hair, smooth skin "like a snake", and "very strong eyes" but had different insides - "no fat, just grease; no blood". He said the sky-country was far away and it was dark and very windy. He was made 'clever by lightning', giving him powers of healing.[22]

The Tiwi of Melville and Bathurst Islands divided their universe into four levels, the underworld, the earth on which they live, the upper world, and beyond that, the sky-world. The upper world had two seasons annually, a wet and a dry. In the dry season, the upper world was the home for the man of thunderstorms, the woman of the monsoonal rains and the woman of lightning. At the end of the dry season, these three moved to the sky-world and, in doing so, shed rain on the dry earth. While this was happening, the trees and plants of the upper world used the raindrops to send their spirits to the ground where they grew into plants. Hence all vegetation on the islands emanated from spirits dropped from the upper world. The sky-world was the place of the stars, the moon and the sun.[23]

The Aranda of Central Australia viewed the sky-world of the ancestors as being a land of natural riches and plenty, with an abundance of

---

22 Rose 1992:94.

23 Roberts and Mountford 1974:66; Sims 1978:166.

food. The linguist Ted Strehlow, who grew up at Hermannsburg with Aranda people, describes a kind of utopia from northern Aranda legends and chant verses.

> Young hunters in the sky-world come home every night weighed down to the limit of their strength with slaughtered wallabies tied together in bundles. The ... men ... "charm" the playful bandicoots by twirling their bull-roarers so that they approach fearlessly and allow themselves to be caught and killed without any attempt to escape from their hunters ... the whole mulga thicket is crowded with peacefully grazing kangaroos ... the banks of the little creek are densely lined with dark green native orange trees, and the gleam of their golden fruit shines far and wide ... Every creek and rill contains water. The plain is green with herbs and grasses; the mountains are decked brightly with a multi-coloured covering of wildflowers. The air is heavy with the scent of eucalypts and acacia buds. Clustering swarms of native bees hum around the pale yellow blossoms of the bloodwood trees, eager to collect the sweet honey. The rocky caves are filled with nimble wallabies; and in the burrows on the plains the sharp-nosed bandicoots are sporting carelessly. Full-throated choirs of cicadas sing in the tall, white-barked rivergums, and their red-golden bodies suffuse the dark foliage of the trees with a bright gleam, as though the gums themselves were all dripping with blood. From the clear sky the eagle swoops down on his shrieking prey when the day stands at high noon; when the shadows of the waning day lengthen out towards the eastern horizon, the euros hop down nimbly from the stone-hills and come down to graze at the edge of the plain. Then the sun covers its face with hair-string ornaments and darkness draws on. The moon comes forth from the mountains, like a proud young man; he wears a chaplet of gleaming white bandicoots' tails; he stands at the edges of a claypan and watches his bright face mirrored in the silver ripples, and is lost in admiration at his own youthful comeliness. In the thick salt-bush the ceaseless plaintive chirp of the lonely cricket is sounding on into the silence of the night; and the emus shake their long

> necks as they come to the rock-holes for a deep cool draught.
> The red plain kangaroos assemble in groups to hold converse
> with their aunts, the mulga parrots.[24]

Furthermore, men and women there never age, 'those above live forever, immortal into all eternity'.[25]

The sky-world was frequently envisaged as containing much quartz crystal and fresh water, both being highly valued resources. There is also an intriguing suggestion that it was represented among New South Wales groups by the Bora Ring of secret initiation grounds.[26] The Dieri of Lake Eyre also described their sky-country as being a beautiful and abundant place, full of trees and birds.[27] It has also been described by some as a 'land of exquisite beauty with flowers blooming everywhere, massed together in brilliant colours like hundreds of rainbows laid out on the grass'. The flowers neither faded nor died. The perception of the sky-world, as an eternal place or space of plenty, beauty and peacefulness was not uncommon.[28]

The Land of the Dead

Over much of Australia and in particular, parts of the west and northwest, the spirits of the dead went to and resided in the sky-world with the ancestral heroes,[29] but as frequently, there was a specially designated earthly place of sojourn for the dead, always located well away from that of the living. Sometimes, it was located at the eastern or western edge of the sky, or on faraway islands. It could be located behind one or more of the fixed stars, as in Arnhem Land where it was held to be

---

24 In Elkin 1976:36–37.

25 Robinson 1966:84–85.

26 Elkin 1976:253.

27 Howitt 1904:358–59.

28 Reed 1985:13–14.

29 Berndt 1974:117.

in a cave on an island behind *Barnumbir*, the morning star.[30] On the island, it is believed that the spirits dance, sending out morning stars to different parts of Arnhem Land. Because the spirits send out their stars attached to strings which they pull in again at dawn, the humans imitate these actions in their mourning rituals. They represent the morning star, using a large pole with feathered strings and balls.[31]

In central and northeast Arnhem Land, mortuary or morning star ceremonies (known as 'sorry business') are performed to ensure the safe passage and transition of the deceased souls to the Land of the Dead. The ceremonies are associated with an ancestral being known as *Wulumumu*, who it was believed, hunted stingrays and gathered yams at Gakulu on Elcho Island. With the vines from the yams, *Wulumumu* made the feather-covered strings that he then attached to the Morning Star, Barnumbir. The feathered strings are believed to guide a person's spirit or soul back to its final resting place. *Wulumumu* is capable of recalling the soul after it has finished its journey across the heavens guided by and attached to the Morning Star. When the Morning Star is seen in the sky, it serves as a form of communication between spirits of deceased ancestors and those still living on the earth.

---

30 The land of the dead is sited in a cave behind the rising sun among the Moil of the Lower Daly River (Worms 1968:169). Among the Kurnai of Eastern Victoria, it was located where the sun touches the western horizon, and could be reached via the rays of the setting sun (Howitt 1904:173). In the Kimberleys, the place of the dead was also in the west (Kaberry 1939:211), and amongst people of the Lower River Murray, it was believed spirits of the dead travelled by a well-defined coastal track and then across the sea to an island (Berndt and Berndt 1974:117). In the eyes of the Kamilaroi of northwest New South Wales, the spirits of the dead go to the Magellanic Clouds (Howitt 1904:431). The Milky Way was also seen as a place of the dead, as in parts of Arnhem Land (Maymuru 1978, Murphy 1991:267–8) and in some areas of the Kimberleys (Durack 1969:242). Amongst the Bibbulmun of Western Australia, the spirits of the dead had to journey under 'father sea', west to the land of the dead (Bates 1992:169).

31 Worms 1968:169.

A deceased person's spirit could also return to a particular place where he or she originated. Amongst the Yarralin[32] for example, one aspect of a person is identified with his or her breath or wind, and when a person dies, life leaves with the wind. If the person dies far away from home, the breath or wind can be seen as a shooting star returning to its own country. If the person dies in his own country, the wind or breath may be associated with a particular star as it passes over to another body to be born again. These people also have a sky-country where the spirits of the dead are people transferred with the aid of ceremonial mourning rituals. The long streaks of light from the setting sun are roads or strings on which the dead travel, escorted by custodians of the dead.

A shooting star also signals death amongst the Kwadji people of eastern Cape York.[33] The people follow the passage of the shooting star across the sky and, if as most often happens, the star merely crosses the sky, they say someone from another area has died, but if a report is heard in conjunction with a shooting star, the people know someone from their own area is dead.

Amongst the Karadjeri in north-western Australia[34] too, shooting stars also indicated death, usually the death of an important man, the direction the shooting star takes indicating where the death had occurred. Amongst the Gundungurra of the Blue Mountains area in New South Wales, the place of the dead was at the end of the sky towards the sea. 'On arrival at the other side (the spirits of the dead) find a large bridge which they cross, and then dive down through a tunnel, at the end of which is a fiery mountain, they pass over this and then meet their friends.'[35]

---

32 Rose 1992:70.

33 Montagu 1974:155.

34 Piddington 1932:394.

35 Feld in Smith 1992:84.

The Nature of Stars

As to the nature of stars themselves, opinions differed. Some Aboriginal groups envisaged them as the tracks, campfires or representations of the sky people. Others saw them as spirits of the dead, and yet others, the Karadjeri[36] for example, thought that, as well as being representations of the spirits of dead men and women, they were globules of light - individual nautilus shells with fish still alive inside them. In this view, shooting stars were seen to be the result of the death of the fish and the discarding of its shell. Every star represented the spirit of some deceased Karadjeri man or woman, while more important stars and even constellations represented objects and persons of myth. Theoretically, all individuals had a place in the sky but the stars to which they corresponded were known only by a few Karadjeri.

Among the Walbiri in the Northern Territory, there was a notion that neighbouring but unknown Mudbara ancestor heroes chopped up the Milky Way, or parts of it, to form the individual stars of the night sky.[37] Amongst the Western Aranda in Central Australia, the stars were seen to be like fires - 'just like fires that glint and gleam as they move along, they hover (above), flashing like lightning as they burn.'[38] In what could well be a humorous throw-away line, the Awabagal of coastal New South Wales were heard to remark that they saw the sun, moon and stars as originating from the head-lice thrown by a man into the fire.[39]

One highly imaginative narrative explains the origin and nature of the stars:

> Beyond the horizon, where no-one has ever been, there is a beautiful land with grassy valleys and tree-covered hills. Streams trickle down the green slopes and join together to form a broad placid river, where flowers nod their heads over

---

36 Piddington 1932:394.

37 Meggitt 1966:124.

38 Robinson 1966:84.

39 Gunson 1974:47.

the banks. The inhabitants of that land are moons - big, shining, globular moons. They have no arms or legs, but they can move quickly across the grass by rolling over and over. It is a pleasant life in that green, watered land, but sometimes the moons grow restless, and when night comes they have the urge to explore farther afield and stroll across the sky. Only one moon ever goes on such a journey at a time ... but ... outside the valley there lives a giant. He catches the wandering moon, and with his flint knife, cuts a slice from it each night, until after many nights there is nothing left but a number of shining slivers. The giant cuts them up very finely and throws them all over the sky. They are timid little creatures, the cut-up moons which have become stars. During the day, when a sun goes striding across the sky, they hide. Who knows but that, if they showed themselves then, another sun might not creep out and catch them unawares. At night there are no suns ... So, in the velvety blackness of the night, they frolic and play until the hungry sun again stamps across the sky.[40]

Ancestral creative spirits having a bird form, which have subsequently become stars is not an uncommon notion. According to Paddy Roe,[41] an Aboriginal elder from the Western Kimberley region, the stars came about after *Djaringgalong*, who was a 'monster bird', stole babies to take home to his nest and eat. Pursuing the babies, two men went to *Djaringgalong's* nest and found two eggs. They consulted with two elders who were healers. They went back to the nest and waited for the monster bird. At dawn he returned. They attacked and speared him and the eggs. The bird subsequently turned into the stars.

A similar ancestral spirit among the Kulin of Victoria[42] is represented as the great eaglehawk, *Bungil*. He was a creative spirit having two wives and a son, *Binbeal*, the rainbow. After he had finished creating the mountains and rivers, the animals and insects, and instructing men, he became tired of earth. So he told *Bellin-bellin*, the crow, to open

---

40 Reed (1965:132) does not locate the place where this story originated.

41 Roe and Muecke 1983:76–82.

42 Massola 1968:109.

the wind which was stored in bags. The wind escaped the bags and blew *Bungil* and his people to the sky where they remain now as stars. From an Arnhem Land[43] myth, *Kakan*, an old hawk, discovers how to make fire by twirling one stick upon another. In a subsequent dispute with a white hawk, the country was set on fire, burning a pine tree which the people have habitually used to climb up to and down from the sky. So the people up in the sky at the time of the fire had to remain. Starlight, as the story goes, comes from the crystals implanted in their heads, elbows, knees and joints.

Stars and the Terrestrial Landscape

The landscape for Aboriginal people was seen as having been created by ancestral spirits and, in many cases, it is still imbued with their presence. Most of the myths which involve the stars have their dramatic starting points or episodes on the earth, so that all over the continent, the terrestrial environment is intrinsically linked with the celestial environment. Many sky-based ancestral heroes and heroines are also associated with particular places on earth.

So, for example, a painted door in the primary school at Yuendumu in Central Australia documents the notion that sacred places on earth fell out of the Milky Way as shooting stars.[44] In another example, Gosse Bluff, also located in Central Australia, is seen as being the result of a group of ancestral women who were dancing across the sky as the Milky Way, when one of them put down her baby in its carrier. The carrier and baby toppled over the edge of the dancing area and both were transformed into a ring of tortured rock walls. To this day the boy's mother and father, as the evening star and the morning star, still search for their child.[45]

---

43 Maddock (1970) in Isaacs 1980105.

44 Warlukurlangu Artists 1987:127.

45 Beale (1994:43) indicates that one scientific explanation for the crater is that the bluff is the site of a direct hit on earth by a comet 130 million

According to the great Bruny Island storyteller, *Wooraddy*, there is a large standing stone behind the great sweeping strand known as Cox Bight on the far south-west of Tasmania. It is the petrified form of *Moinee*, an important creator-ancestor who cut the rivers and cleaved the land of *Trowenna*, the place we now call Tasmania. *Moinee*, originally a gleaming white star, was a boy born to *Parnuen*, the sun, and his wife *Vena*, the moon. *Moinee* created the first human being, but his brother *Dromerdene* intervened to remodel the human's anatomy. So furious was *Moinee* at this intervention that he fought a tremendous battle in the heavens with *Dromerdene*. As a result, *Dromerdene* tumbled into the sea and *Moinee* fell to earth, his landfall being in the far south-west, where he then lived as a man.[46]

At Glen Helen Gap in the western MacDonnell Ranges the stories associated with Orion and the Pleiades are represented in the rocks. The man of Orion pursued the women of the Pleiades to these rocks where they are clustered together in fright, desperately hoping that he would not see them. The women have since been transformed into the rocks which cling to the side of the Finke Gorge. The oldest sister took up a position where she could watch *Nirunja's* (Orion's) movements, and her body is now a spectacular outcrop of vertically bedded rocks. Despite the oldest sister's precautions, however, the man of Orion captured and raped one of the women. At the mouth of the Glen Helen Gorge, there are rows of vertically bedded rocks. It is thought that these were created by the feet of the dancing Pleiades-women as they performed a women's ceremony.[47]

There is a myriad of these associations, between celestial objects and particular terrestrial places spread far and wide across the Australian landscape. In Queensland, in the Tully area, a rather bare place known as Green Hill (between Gordonvale and the sea) is thought to be the site

---

years ago which would have changed the whole planet like a bell. It left a crater 20 kilometres wide, the walls of which have eroded by more than 2000 metres.

46 Plomley 1956:118.

47 Mountford 1976b:480–82.

where, long ago, the moon *(Carcurrah)*, feeling dizzy, fell from its place in the heavens. It skimmed over the thick forest, from the top of the hill down into a large swamp and there it lay, held tight despite the pulling and shoving of the many animals around. So exhausted were they that they left the moon to its fate. Enraged at being deserted, *Carcurrah* called out a vengeful curse: 'Henceforth, one of you shall die every second year. All the birds and animals who live near Redbank, Wright's Creek and Yatee Station shall suffer the same fate, and never more shall the trees grow on the Green Hill.' And so it happened, goes the story. [48]

There has been speculation about the possibility of ground recordings of celestial maps throughout the country. On the Elvina Track at West Head in the Kur-ring-gai Chase National Park, for example, there is a tesselated rock platform marked by holes, which may well represent the position of astronomical bodies. According to Stanbury and Clegg (1990), Cairns (1993), and Cairns and Branagan (1992), the whole area may be a celestial map. Cairns and Branagan go so far as to assert that, based on ethnographic accounts,[49] 'cognitive intellectual mapping' did occur. Moreover argues Cairns, 'abstract physical mapping of lunar phase(s) complemented by isomorphic representation of star patterns' was likely and could well be found in rock engravings and paintings. This is clearly a possibility, but at this stage, is still speculative.[50]

---

48 Henry 1967:38.

49 By the Berndts, Dawson, Elkin, Howitt, Mountford, Roth and Strehlow.

50 Cairns 1993:148–49.

3

Natural Cycles and the Stars

Seasonal Calendars

Aboriginal and Torres Strait Islander peoples' knowledge of the interdependence of natural systems and cycles is, fortunately, quite well documented. One such account comes from George Augustus Robertson, a one-time Chief Protector of Aborigines, who regularly camped out with Tasmanian Aboriginal people during the 1830s. He reported that he had a deep respect for the Aboriginal people's ability to read the clouds, the moon and the stars, thereby forecasting the weather in one of the most changeable climates in Australia.

'I have seldom seen them to err', he wrote in one of his numerous reports.[1] This particular facility was also noted among groups in western Victoria:

> great reliance is placed by the natives on certain signs, as indicating a change in the weather ... They notice the appearance of the sun, moon, stars and clouds, the cries and movements of animals, etc. A bright sunrise prognosticates fine weather, a red sunrise, rain; a red sunset, heat next day; a halo around the sun, fine weather; a bright moon, fine weather; the old moon in the arms of the new, rain; the new moon lying on its back, dry weather; a halo around the moon, rain; a rainbow in the morning, fine weather; a rainbow in the evening, bad weather; a rainbow during rain, clearing up; when mosquitoes and gnats are very troublesome, rain is expected; when the cicada sings at night, there will be a hot wind next day ... They believe that, in dry weather, if any influential person takes water into his [sic] mouth, and blows it towards the

---

1 Quoted in Blainey 1975:22.

> setting sun, saying 'Come down, rain', the wind will blow and
> the rain will pour for three days.[2]

Of such importance was a knowledge of the stars in denoting the particular seasons of the year, that it was considered to be one of the principal branches of education.[3] In some parts of the continent, contemporary management strategies have been put into place taking this knowledge and experience into account. The depth and detail of this knowledge best shows in localised contexts. There is great diversity in natural phenomena that give clues to seasonal change, which in turn determine the timing of activities and changing foci of social, economic, domestic and ceremonial practices.

Aboriginal people traditionally had no methods for accurately measuring and recording the annual circuit of the sun, but various indices were chosen to indicate the progression of time and season. Cairns[4] hypothesises that message sticks and rock engraving could have been used to record the timing of ceremonies, tribal meetings, menstruation and gestation cycles, but evidence is sparse and controversial. Yet the changing parade of stars and star patterns was a clear and well-recognised index of seasonal changes at least. 'The appearance of certain constellations heralds or coincides with particular terrestrial events and is in some cases believed to be responsible for them.'[5]

The northern aspects of any Australian night sky show a changing order of stars, whereas the southern aspects show the same stars but in differing positions because of Australia's apparent location beneath a revolving south celestial pole. 'When the rising of a star is expected (on the Torres Strait Islands), it is the duty of the old men to watch. They get up when the birds begin to cry and watch till daybreak... The setting of a star is watched in the same way.'[6]

---

2 Dawson 1981:98.

3 Dawson 1981:99.

4 Cairns 1993:140, 145.

5 Lowe and Pike 1990:110.

6 Rivers in Haddon et al 1912(4):224.

Food gathering and hunting locations and practices changed according to the seasons. The Victorian Mallee Aboriginal people, for example, knew by the appearance in the northern sky of the star known to Europeans as Arcturus (*Alpha Bootis*) that the prized larvae of the wood-ant were coming into season. When Arcturus, known as *Marpeankurrk*, set with the sun, the larvae were finished.[7] This observation was also tied to a notion that *Marpeankurrk* was an ancestor who originally discovered the larvae and after death became a star in order that she could indicate to the people when the larvae were coming into season. The appearance at sunrise of Arcturus was also a signal in Millingimbi in Arnhem Land and indicated that the spike thrush (*rakia*)—a type of water chestnut (*eleocharis* sp.)—was ready for collection.[8] The availability of this same corm or groundnut was signalled differently just a few kilometres further east.

In north-east Arnhem Land, the 'lily star' (planet Venus to Europeans) when low in the western sky just after sunset indicated the time of the *rakia*. The pied magpie-geese with their hard hooked beaks also came in flocks to feed on these groundnuts, so they became easily available food to the local Aboriginal people, who moved in family groups to the plains near the sea. The corms of the spike thrush were also softened considerably when they were taken directly from the gullets of the pied geese. Many Aboriginal groups joined together on the coastal plains to enjoy the profusion of food. As a result, it also became a time for mutual ritual activity.[9] In the south, Vega (*Alpha Lyra*) was significant to the Boorong people of the Victorian Mallee, as it indicated when the mallee-hen's eggs are available for collection (during October) as food.[10]

---

7 Massola 1971:44, Stanbridge (1857) in MacPherson 1881:72.

8 Mountford 1956:495.

9 Wells 1973:21–30.

10 Stanbridge (1857) in MacPherson 1881:72.

Other fragments suggest that Aboriginal people of eastern New South Wales[11] (particularly around the Clarence River)[12] as well as groups in the Western Desert [13] saw the Pleiades, (see Diagram 1) when appearing in the east early in the evening, as heralding warm weather. When this open star cluster set with the sun, people of the Western desert saw it as a temporary departure, leaving only for the winter. Its heliacal rising coincided with the coming of the dingo pups and marked the beginning of a new cycle (late autumn). The cycle began with the cold weather, then dry times, followed by hot times and then the time of the rains, which were generally regarded as 'the good time'. In 'good times', camps with a good view, on soft ground without prickles, near supplies of firewood, could be set up almost anywhere. Water was abundant, with claypans and other temporary storages being full. Everything was green and growing in lush abundance. After rains, all old tracks were washed away and every new track was a fresh mark on a clean sheet, so animal tracking was much easier. The coming of the dingo pups came earlier in Arnhem Land, and Orion rising at dawn (about June) signalled this propitious event.[14]

The Pleiades, when they were in the sky before dawn in the Great Sandy Desert of Western Australia, were seen as a signal of the onset of the coldest nights. According to local myth, the Pleiades women dropped water on the people sleeping below, causing them to shiver with cold.[15] This is much the same for the Adnyamatana people of the Flinders Ranges of South Australia. At this time (July), they also signified *malkada*-time, the time of initiation for boys[16]. A similar tradition existed among the Aranda and Luritja groups of Central Australia. Here they were seen as a group of women and were also associated with

---

11 Massola 1971:44.

12 Mathews 1905:77–78.

13 Tindale in Hiatt 1978:158–159.

14 Elkin 1974:32.

15 Lowe and Pike 1990:110.

16 Tunbridge 1988:16.

frost.[17] Among the Muruwuri people from inland New South Wales and Queensland border areas (as with their Western Desert counterparts), the Pleiades, when rising about three hours before dawn, were seen to be women who urinated regularly creating ice (or frost) before sunrise.[18] The Adnyamatana people in South Australia viewed the Pleiades women as having a pouch like that of the kangaroo. The pouch was believed to be filled with fine white frost crystals which streamed from the women as they crossed the sky.[19]

When the constellation known to Europeans as Scorpius (see Diagram 3) attained a particular position in the night sky, the people of Groote Eylandt knew that the wet season was about to cease and the south-easterlies were due.[20] When it was high in the early morning sky, people at Yirrkala knew that the Malay fishermen would soon arrive on their yearly visit to collect trepang (sea cucumbers).[21]

A most explicit example of the coordination of seasonal activities and star cycles is recorded by Sharp (1993). Her detailed study of the Meriam people of the eastern Torres Strait indicates the great significance of star knowledge and of one constellation in particular. *Tagai* (or *Togai*) is a mythical ancestral hero who belongs to all Torres Strait Islanders. He is represented in the night sky as an island-man and is envisaged as standing in a canoe. In his left hand, he holds a fishing spear, the three-pronged head of which is represented by the Southern Cross (*Crux Australis*). In his right hand, he holds an apple-like fruit, known as a Eugenia, represented by the constellation of the Crow (Corvus). The vast constellation of *Tagai* consists of the European constellations of Sagittarius, part of Telescopium, Scorpius, Lupus, Centaurus, the Southern Cross, Corvus, part of Hydra and one star of Ara. *Tagai* himself is composed of Centaurus and Lupus (his eyes

---

17 Strehlow 1907:23–24.

18 Mathews 1982:13–14.

19 Mountford 1939:103–104.

20 Mountford 1956:94.

21 Mountford 1956:504.

are *Gamma* and *Mu Centauri, Phi Centauri* is his chin, *Eta Centauri* is his navel, and *Kappa Centauri* and *Beta Lupi* are his testes). He stands in front of his canoe which consists of the body and tail of Scorpius, the canoe's anchor is represented by Sagittarius and part of Scorpius and Telescopium is a sucker-fish below the canoe (see Diagram 2 and Drawing 1). In addition, there are twelve crewmen, six of whom are represented by the Pleiades group and the other six represented by the stars in the belt of Orion.[22] The rhythm of the Meriam people's lives followed the movement through the night skies of this large constellation. The stars of *Tagai* ushered in seasonal and ceremonial changes and acted as a guide to voyaging, cultivation and fishing.

The myth itself tells the story of *Tagai* and his twelve crewmen who consisted of *Usiam* (the Pleiades), and *Seg* (the three stars in the belt of Orion) (see Diagram 1). These crewmen stole the food and drink which had been prepared for a voyage. As a result, they were all thrown overboard into the sea by *Tagai*, their images set into star patterns forever.

The *Seasonal Calendar* of Meriam life reflected the changes in the seas, the winds, the stars and the land, and moved through cycles of abundance and scarcity, renewal and harvest, wet and dry. As island cultures (there are three islands - Mer, Daua and Waier), dependent on sedentary agriculture and fishing, they allowed the winds and tides to set the pace. Seasonal changes dictated the social agendas in Meriam life: differing food availability affected diets, activities changed and variations in mood, hopes and expectations were the lot of everyone.

There were four main seasonal times - *kerker-naiger, koki, ziai* and *sager* - each closely associated with the prevailing winds (see *Seasonal Calendar* following). Mid *naiger* (early October) began the cycle, when the constellation of *Tagai* rose in the east. Firstly at dusk, *Usiam* (the Pleiades) with *Seg* (Orion's belt) nearby, appeared in the north-east sky. *Usiam*-time (Pleiades-time) was the time of planting. It was regarded as a time of renewal, of re-beginning. It also marked the commencement of the ritual cycle, when, after preparations, voyaging expeditions to the Papuan mainland, other islands and Cape York took place for

---

22 Sharp 1993:3,4; Rivers in Haddon 1912:219.

commodity and ritual exchanges. At the same time, a star known as *abud wer*[23] signalled the approach of the first rains. When the Southern Cross (*Crux Australis*) found the left hand of *Tagai*, it signalled to the gardeners that it was time to plant important yam varieties. Before the complete appearance of *Tagai*, garden preparations should have been completed.

In December, a total stillness and the appearance of a rainbow-like sunset signalled the arrival of *koki kerker*, generally a time of heavy rains, during which there was luxuriant growth. Planting continued using the tides and the moon to indicate the most propitious times. The prescriptive schedule indicated that when the tide was rising and flooding, planting should have been done and when the tide dropped, planting stopped. At new moon, vegetables that fruit above ground should be planted, and at full moon, plants with root food that grows down should be planted. When the full moon rises, sweet potato should be planted, making sure that it is positioned facing towards the full moon. The people took up residence in round houses on family lands along the sandy beaches for extra protection against the rains. Although vegetable products were scarce, bananas and coconuts were available, and fishing was very good, especially in the fish traps prepared by the people earlier in the cycle. Birds were hunted, particularly the frigate bird and the tern.

As the rains ceased with the cooler weather, it was *ziai kerker* (the month of March). It was signalled by the winds turning around to the south. Early vegetable foods were harvested and fishing yields were high.

Sager kerker was signalled when the rainbow fish appeared and the kingfisher returned to the islands in early April. Harvesting began in earnest, particularly of the yam, thirty varieties of which were grown by the Meriam people. The planet Venus was the sign of the height of the harvest. Fish continued to be plentiful. Eugenia, the red-skinned apple-like fruit (Corvus in *Tagai*'s right hand), fruited and local ceremonies and feast offerings between reciprocal clans began. *Sager kerker*

---

23 Not specified by Sharp.

also heralded the approach of one phase of the three-yearly cycle of rites of *Malo* (an ancestral hero of ecological significance). These rituals involved initiation ceremonies and preparation rites for maritime expeditions or *wauri*. The dances of the *Malo* rites symbolised the waves that would carry the voyagers, as friends of *Malo*, safely onto other places. This season was one of replenishment, when grass-vine and bamboo-thatched house-building and maintenance took place. Tools, weapons, fishing lines and nets were renewed and repaired.

As the weather became drier and hotter from August onward, the early *naiger kerker* announced itself, especially when the turtles began mating. Fishing was poor and vegetables were scarce. Garden preparation, using slash and burn techniques took place, as well as preparation activities, including outrigger-canoe maintenance, for *wauri* voyages.

The *Seasonal Calendar* of the easterly based Meriam people makes an interesting comparison with the more westerly situated people of the islands of Mabuiag and Muralag in the Torres Strait.[24] There were four main seasons - *surlal, raz, kuki* and *aibaud* (see *Seasonal Calendar* following).

Surlal (mid-October to late November) began the yearly cycle and took its name from the readily caught copulating turtles, indicating their abundance as food. The *baidam* or 'shark constellation', which consisted of the seven major stars of Ursa Major together with Arcturus (*Alpha Bootis*) and *Gamma Corona Borealis*, appeared low in the evening sky close to the reef (see Drawing 3). It was the dry season and all was withered and dried up. The yams harvested in the previous season were still available for eating. The sounding of the first thunder acted to signal the time for re-planting of the many varieties of yams.

Raz (early December to late February) was described as the 'time of die', meaning the season when leaves died down. Early in the season cashew nuts fell and young yams began to sprout. The winds shifted around readily. In mid-season, large numbers of jellyfish appeared and the runners on the yams began to grow.

---

24 As discussed by Rivers and Ray in Haddon 1912(4):26–28.

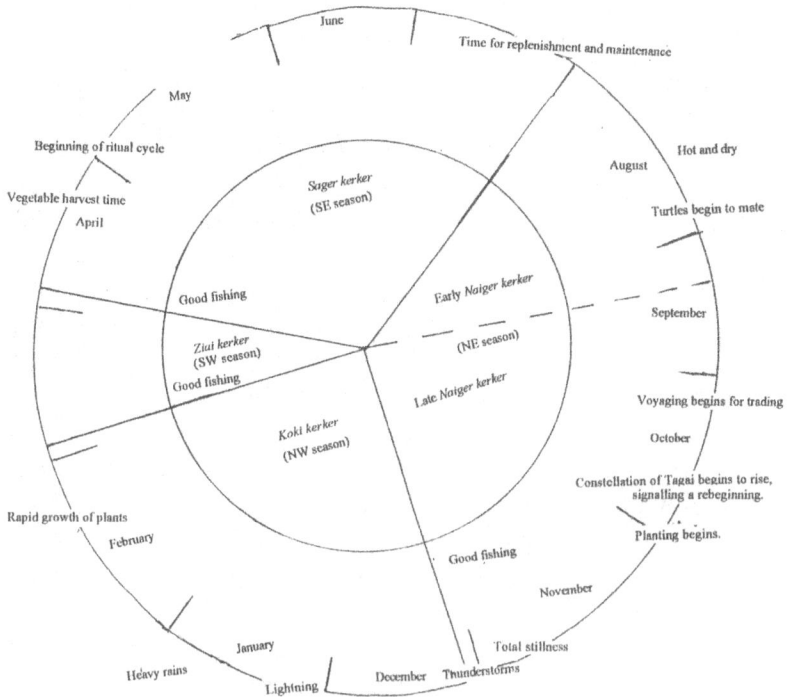

Seasonal Calendar of the Meriam People (based on information in Sharp 1993).

Kuki (early March to mid May) was the season when strong winds blew intermittently from the north-west, accompanied by deluges of rain. During the intervals between storms, there was no wind and the seas became calm and glassy. It was very humid. The yams were not ready to eat so vegetables such as *kolap* (Queensland bean) were eaten. The appearance of Altair (*Alpha Aquilae*), *Beta* and *Gamma Aquilae* (part of the *Dogai*, a female bogey constellation) heralded the beginning of the season. The appearance of the constellation *bu*, 'the trumpet shell' (Delphinus) was also significant (see Drawing 4). According to one Mabuiag man, '*Dogai* go first, *bu* come after. When *bu* go down blow comes, wind not strong.'[25]

Aibaud (late May to early October) was the harvest season, when roots were strong and food (especially taro, sweet potato and wild yam) was abundant. The south-west wind began to blow steadily. The season was marked by the appearance of Vega (*Alpha Lyrae*), *Beta* and *Gamma Lyrae*, also part of the *Dogai* constellation. The appearance of a star known as *kek* [26] (see Drawing 2) signalled the time for the performance of various ceremonies. According to one Mabuiag man, '*Kek* come up and is sign (*mek*) for everything to be done, start meeting'. *Dideal* [27] and *Usal* (the Pleiades) also appeared. When the crab, *Getalar* appeared,[28] the *birubiru* birds migrated from Papua New Guinea south to Australia, as did the Torres Strait pigeons when *baidam*, the shark constellation (see Drawing 3), appeared heralding the beginning of another cycle. When only the tail of *baidam* was above the horizon, the north-west wind began to blow 'a little bit', but when the tail had gone down altogether, it was time to begin to plant yams. When *baidam* came up again, yams, sweet potatoes and bananas were known to have ripened.

Tagai or *Togai* was also significant in the more westerly islands of the Torres Strait (see Drawings 5 and 6). Legend had it that *Togai* and his brother *Koang* were sent out in a canoe to get turtle-shell for their (maternal) nephew *Kwoiam*. Both brothers could make fine weather but *Togai* excelled. On this particular voyage, the crew consisted of *Utimal* (probably the stars in Orion's belt), *Usal* (the Pleiades) *Kwoior* (star not determined) and *Keg* or *Kek* (Achernar). These men stole the water belonging to *Koang* and *Togai*. On a subsequent voyage, they were killed in revenge. The two old brothers told the dead men '*Usal*, you go to New Guinea (*Daudai*) side, when you come up there will be plenty of rain. *Utimal*, you go to New Guinea side, you have to bring rain. *Kwoior*,

---

25 In discussion with Rivers.

26 Probably Achernar (*Alpha Eridai*), according to Rivers.

27 Probably Orion, according to Rivers.

28 Probably a nebula, suggests Rivers.

different stars when you come up over *Buru* (Mangrove Island) just before the south-east monsoon sets in there will be rain in the morning, then the wind will shift and it will rain in the afternoon. And you, *Kek*, will come up in the south between *Badu* and *Moa*, and it will be cold weather. When you go round this way and when you come up, then the yams and sweet-potatoes will be ripe. You all have work to do.'[29] The legend showed how these dead men were transformed into stars, their task being to usher in certain seasonal changes when they first appeared on the eastern horizon.

This notion of different stars ushering in different seasons (months or moons) is consistent with beliefs and ritual practices amongst the Kiwai Papuans in the Gulf District of Papua New Guinea.[30] There, *Tagai* (originally a Mabuiag or Saibai man from the Torres Strait) and his sons or younger brothers went spear-fishing. The youngest son or brother *Karongo* was reputed to be an idle fellow, behaviour which particularly irritated the other sons or brothers. *Tagai* finally became angry and speared *Karongo* hurling him into the sky to become Antares saying: 'You go down along ground (set below the horizon) first, before north-west he start blow'. Still in a rage, *Tagai* speared the others as well.

The next son or brother killed became Wega (Vega): 'Time belong you, you give him plenty fish, fine water all time'. And the next was turned into Atair (Altair), *Tagai* saying to him, 'Brother belong you, he give fish, you give plenty fish too. People no can sleep inside house, sleep underneath house, because belly he full, wind he no blow inside house, too hot'. The fourth son or brother was not designated a star, only a month (or moon); *Tagai* said to him, 'You belong blow, north-west he blow, rain wind; no give no chance (blows incessantly)'. The fifth became *Keke* (Achernar), *Tagai* saying 'I chuck away you, you go head he come up, you make him that wind blow'. The sixth son or brother became *Utiamo* (the Pleiades) with the ultimatum 'You fellow belong south-east, more south-east'. The next became Orion with 'You fellow belong south-east, more south-east he blow, no give chance (it blows

---

29 Rivers in Haddon et al 1912 (4):26.

30 Landtman 1917:482–484.

incessantly). The last crewman became Capella, Sirius and Canopus: 'More south-east he come, you make him come more blow, rain, wind make him more cold'.

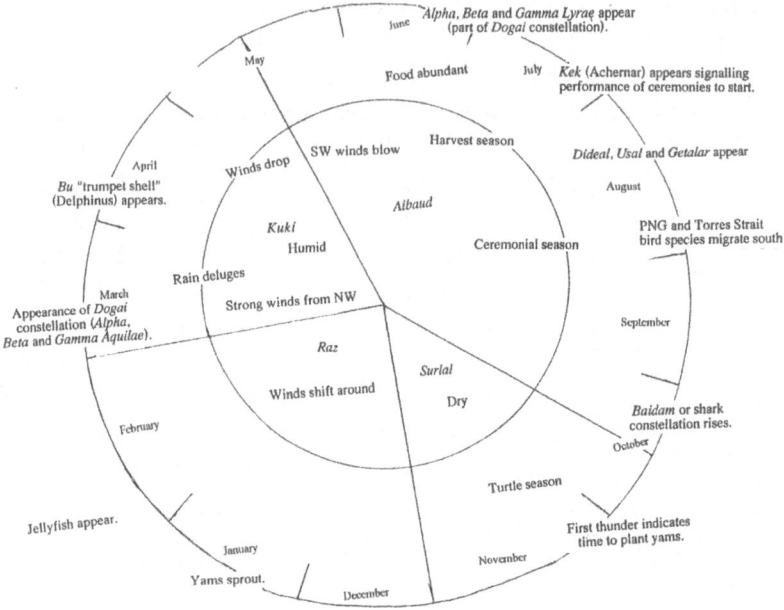

Seasonal Calendar of the Mabuiag and Muralag Island People (Rivers and Ray Haddon et al. 1912 [4] [5]).

Having killed off all his crew, *Tagai* himself became the Southern Cross. He met his sons or brothers and said to them all, 'Me go first, you follow behind me. I make him wind blow first, behind (then) you fellow make him'. Ursa Major was considered to be the shape of the shark (*Baidamu*) and also part of *Tagai*'s crew. *Tagai* was reputed to have said to him: 'That time fin belong you go down, more wind, more high water he come. Tail belong you he go down: make more high water. Head belong you come up, make plenty "fast turtle" (the copulating season of the turtles comes in). Look sundown: Oh, that star he no more stop, he been go away. Wait two, three day, look before daylight:

Oh, head belong Baidamu come up morning time'. The final star in the narrative was the morning star, to whom *Tagai* said: 'You come first, daylight come behind, you stand up close to daylight'. In one account of the myth, *Tagai* himself went up to the sky as a shooting star. His month (about October) is very hot and dry.

Another *Seasonal Calendar* of interest is the Gagadju (Kakadu) cycle (see *Seasonal Calendar* following). This particular seasonal model has been taken up by the Australian National Parks and Wildlife Department in its Management Plan of the Kakadu National Park.

In the coastal lowlands of the East Alligator River, there are six seasons - *gunumeleng* (October to December), *gudjewg* (January to March), *bang-gereng* (April), *yegge* (May-June), *wurrgeng* (June-July) and *gurrung* (August-September).[31] Movements of the people in this area are initiated by changes in food supply, comfort and ceremonial ritual, all of which are directly influenced by seasonal change.

Gunumeleng is the extremely hot and humid pre-monsoon season. Winds swing around wildly and storm clouds build up. Waterholes and billabongs dry up and the mud cracks. As the drought is broken by fierce thunderstorms and lightning, insects and frogs, reptiles, birds and mammals are fattened on the new plant growth. The Bunitj people move their camps away from the flood plains.

Gudjewg is the monsoon season, the 'big wet'. The wetlands fill and spring-tides move over the lowlands. There are no electrical storms, just prolonged, heavy rain and strong winds. There is an abundance of growth, and a profuse flowering. Lorikeets swarm over flowering eucalypts, magpie geese nestle in sedgeland and barramundi move into the grasses making them easy to spear. Other fish are plentiful and mangrove worms are deliciously fat.

Bang-Gereng is the season of light winds. There is still much water on the lowland areas and creeks run clear and profusely from sandstone. Most plants are fruiting and animals have given birth to their young. The end of the seasons is marked by a change in the flattening of

---

31 Outlined by Bill Neidjie of the Bunitj clan, Gagadju language group, Neidjie et al 1985:18–23.

the native sorghum, giving the season its other name of 'season of the knock-em-down storms'.

Yegge is the season when nights grow cooler and it is frequently misty in the early mornings. Winds blow constantly from the south-east, drying out the grasslands. Fires near campsites and green feed areas are lit, and the masses of insects which move before the fires are preyed upon by kites and wood-swallows. Many birds fly south as the season begins to dry out. Snakes and flying foxes are particularly favoured foods of the Bunitj people at this time of the cycle.

Wurrgeng is the cold weather time. Estuary food, mud and fiddler crabs become important and barramundi and mullet move into the more settled waters as the south-east wind picks up. Fires burn by day and heavy dews fall at night.

Gurrung is the time when the south-east winds warm the land, as the hot-dry season begins. The pandanus fruit ripen, snakes lay their eggs and when the stringybark flowers, honey is in abundance. Sharks and rays are fat and turtles lay their eggs on the sandy beaches. Well-fed emus, brolga, magpie geese, bandicoots and wallabies are hunted as food. The bush is dry and smoky as the thunderheads build up.

And so it happened that 'geography and seasonality ruled Aboriginal lives through their effect on access and food supply ... not so much controlling the shortage of food but the maintenance of variety. Seasonal changes usher in new foods'.[32]

Again, it would appear particular stars signalled the seasonal changes for, according to Neidjie, whose Gagadju forebears have inhabited the area continuously for the last 25 000 years: 'I look at star, I know just about time for wet season / may be time for dry season / I know from star. Well now that star over here, so look out for wet season. That star right down in December. When that wet come, that star come back. I say "Well, dry season coming". The rain finish him up. October ... up high. November ... getting low. December ... right down'.[33]

---

32 Fox in Neidjie et al 1985:25.

33 Neidjie (1985:55) does not indicate the particular stars to which he is referring.

Seasonal Calendar of the Gagadju People (based on information in Neidjie et al., 1993).

With the change in seasons, came the movement in the people's lives:

All these places for us ... all belong Gagadju. We use them all the time. Old people used to move around, camp different places. Wet season, dry season ... always camp different place. Wet season ... we camp high place, get plenty goose egg. No trouble for fresh water. Dry season ... move along floodplain, billabong got plenty food. Even food there when everything dry out. All Gagadju used to visit ... used to come here to bill-abong ... dry season camp. Plenty file snake, long-neck turtle. Early dry season ... good lily. Just about middle dry season ... file snake, long-neck turtle, lily flowering. Everybody camp,

53

like holiday. Plenty food this place. Good time for ceremony, stay maybe one or two weeks.[34]

Another example of a *Seasonal Calendar* comes from the Yarralin people of the Victoria River Valley in the Northern Territory. In this version, the lower atmosphere phenomenon of the rainbow acts as the signal to seasonal change and is associated with all manifestations of water and water resources. The seasons themselves are conceptualised as being the actions of the sun, the winds and the Rainbow Snake. Deborah Bird Rose explains:

> At this time (the late dry season - October and November) the earth has become so hot that it can hurt people's feet to walk on bare soil. the wind is blowing from the south-east - hot, dry and dusty. the country is parched, the animals have grown thin, the waterholes and billabongs are drying up. The sun, which is necessary to life, is beginning to destroy life ... As the blossoms (of the open savannah eucalypts) dry up, the flying foxes move to the river, roosting in the trees along the permanent waterholes. When the Rainbow snakes see the flying foxes, their Dreaming allies, hanging above them, they know it is time to move.

> Now the rainbow is young and restless. It gets up out of the water, opens its mouth, and shoots out lightning and saliva. The saliva is rain and it contains tadpoles. The first rain alerts the lightning people. Lightning women flash their lightning with ever-increasing frequency, aroused by the Rainbow snake. The rain brings steam up from the hot earth; steam collects into clouds which carry more rain. Tadpoles turn into frogs who sit up and call for more rain. The wind shifts, coming now from the north-west.

> These early rains arouse other species. Various grubs, as well as frogs, are "boss" for rain: they call on the rainbow to bring more. As the rain increases, the floodwaters rise, signalling the presence of the mature rainbow. The water becomes dark

---

34 Neidjie et al 1985:41–42.

and muddy, forming whirlpools which are the rainbow in action. Careless people and animals can be sucked into these pools, drowned and perhaps eaten by the rainbows.

After a few months the rainbow has expanded its influence enormously: floods abound, the sky has been cloudy for a long time; the sun has been eclipsed by the rain. The flying foxes are said to have gone underwater to join the rainbow, and frogs stop calling for rain. The rainbow has been roaming abroad and is becoming "old and tired".

The sun now asserts itself, burning the rainbow. At the same time, the wind shifts to the east and breaks the rainbow's back. Burnt and broken, it retreats to the rivers. The east wind clears the skies and brings up cold weather. Dingoes and their litters, kangaroos and turkeys become fat; the whole emphasis of the world shifts from water to land, from rain to sun, from river resources to land resources. When the country dries out, the white gum trees blossom and the flying foxes return. Cold weather recedes as the sun takes over the sky and heats up the earth, and the whole cycle begins again.

It is curious that despite severe extremes in the cycle, the Yarralin people view the country as a land of abundance and plenty for those who know how to use it. Predation on various species, for example, depends on precise knowledge about their particular ecosystem, as well as how much food they already had, how many people there were to feed at any time, what the condition was of the animal or plant population and whether the animal or plant was restricted because of its perceived relation as their 'countrymen' or 'flesh'.[35]

Among the more southerly Yaraldi (Jaralde) of the Murray River and Lakes region of South Australia, four seasons are distinguished: *riwuri* (spring), the time of growth and mating from August to October; *Iuwadang* (summer), the time of warmth from November to January; *marangani* or *marangalkadi* (autumn), the time of the Crow from

---

35 Rose 1992:100.

February to April; and *yutang* (winter), the time of the cold from May to July[36] (see *Seasonal Calendar* following).

The 'red star' Mars (*Waiyungari*, a mythical ancestor who eloped with the two wives of another great ancestor, *Nepeli*) was seen to be responsible for spring and personified sexual activity and fertility. *Waiyungari* was also the 'patron of all hunting' and therefore the object of ritual activity. *Marangani* was the name of the Crow, also an important mythological figure, regarded as being propitious for fishing and responsible for the ebb and flow of tides, and one whose season coincided with the juxtaposition of certain stars. During the coldest time, the people retreated into huts with skin cloaks and rugs. It was envisaged that the Crow spent little of his time in the sky, so busy was he in the huts of various women. When the people considered that the westerly winds should have abated, the old men would go out and examine the moon: if it appeared clearly, they knew the gales would soon recede.

Another significant group of stars known as 'the young men and girls' appeared in September and October and disappeared in March-April. During this time, the particular star clusters drew closer together and were said to be 'playing together'.[37] The husband and wife anthropologists, Berndt and Berndt, comment that 'while this was regarded as mirroring the normal association of males and females, it also symbolised the antithetical nature of that relationship which served as an interruptive influence on the initiatory sequence'.[38] The seasons, then, are associated with the appearance and disappearance of mythological heroes and heroines represented as stars, whose interwoven stories link

---

36 Berndt and Berndt 1993:76.

37 The particular star clusters involved are not clearly designated but could well be NGC 2516 and NGC 2351.

38 Berndt and Berndt 1993:164.

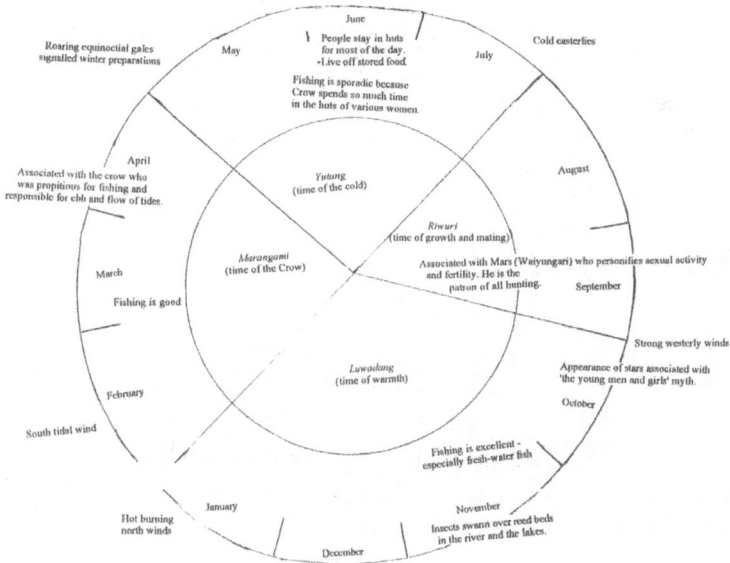

Diagram labels (clockwise from top):

June
People stay in huts for most of the day. -Live off stored food.
July
Cold easterlies
Fishing is sporadic because Crow spends so much time in the huts of various women.
Roaring equinoctial gales signalled winter preparations
May
April
Associated with the crow who was propitious for fishing and responsible for ebb and flow of tides.
August
Yutang (time of the cold)
Riwuri (time of growth and mating)
Marangami (time of the Crow)
Associated with Mars (Waiyungari) who personifies sexual activity and fertility. He is the patron of all hunting.
September
March
Fishing is good
Strong westerly winds
Luwadang (time of warmth)
Appearance of stars associated with 'the young men and girls' myth.
October
February
South tidal wind
Fishing is excellent - especially fresh-water fish
January
Hot burning north winds
November
Insects swarm over reed beds in the river and the lakes.
December

Seasonal Calandar of the Yaraldi (Jaralde) People (based on information in Berndt and Berndt, 1993).

The Karadjeri of north-western Western Australia also had a very extensive star mythology.[39] Most of the more important stars were regarded as the *bilyur* (spirits) of characters described in the myths. The myths were associated with seasonal change and in some cases, mythical creatures were causally connected to the changes. The change of season from dry to wet for example, was seen to be affected by *bulian*, a great water-serpent.[40] The eyes of *bulian* were seen to be two stars in the sky. And if *bulian* was annoyed, it was thought that he would produce change prematurely. 'The special association of the latter end of the dry season, and also the wet season, with *bulian* is expressed in the star mythology; all the stars representing *bulian* are clearly visible

39 Recorded by Piddington 1930:353.

40 A manifestation of the Rainbow Serpent, an important creation spirit across the continent.

at this time of the year.'[41] The stars in Scorpius were also associated with *bulian* but set earlier, during the hot-dry season. This change in season took place in mid-December and was regarded as being very significant because it altered economic and social life to a great extent. There was usually no rain from May to December and after that, heavy rains fell during January and February.

Marine Navigation

As Australian Aboriginal people were primarily hunters and gatherers, they were land based. However fishing, both ocean and river, for many groups provided important dietary components either as a staple or as a supplement. Knowledge of tides and winds as well as seasons was obviously significant for the successful preparation and undertaking of this activity especially if fish traps or canoes were used.

Sailing and voyaging by canoe, in one form or another, was also extremely important to some groups of Aboriginal people, clearly indicated by their having projected a canoe into the sky, represented by stars. Among the Lower River Murray people in South Australia, a mythical canoe no longer used on earth was thought to have been lifted up and placed in the Milky Way.[42] At Millingimbi and Yirrkala in Arnhem Land, all the stars of Orion, the Hyades, the Pleiades and those between these European constellations (see Diagram 3) were included in the Aboriginal constellation of *Tjilulpuna* known also as 'the canoe stars'. It is visible during the wet season. The *tjilulpuna* (fishermen) in the canoe (Orion) and their wives (the Pleiades) in a separate canoe were all out at sea, and when nearing Cape Arnhem, it is thought, a heavy storm swamped both the canoes and drowned all the people. The two canoes, the men, the women, turtle, fish and a whale they had caught, are now in the sky.[43]

41 Piddington 1930:353.

42 Berndt and Berndt 1977:203.

43 Mountford 1956:493,498–500.

In north east Arnhem Land[44] there are two (unnamed) stars which are significant to navigators. These two stars are seen in myth as two fisherman-brothers, the elder of whom drowned while saving his younger brother. These stars are perceived to be spirit-guardians of the men who go out in canoes. When these stars present themselves as a shadow on the sea during the day or as a soft light on the water during the night, the fishermen out in their canoes read these as early warnings of coming storms. They turn into shore well before the ensuing thunder and winds.

For the people of the Torres Strait, the canoe of the hunter and spear-fisherman *Tagai*, is represented by the European constellation of Scorpius (see Drawings 5 and 6). Living in an island-sea culture, the Meriam people identify with the sea and perceive themselves as 'blue-water people'. Much energy goes into the preparation for voyages by outrigger-canoe to other islands for the purpose of exchange. The most significant aspect of the exchange is the *wauri*, shell armlets made from cone shell (*Conus millepunctatus*). These shell armlets are ritually given between exchange partners and, at their peak, the *wauri* exchanges resemble the *kula* of the Trobriand Islands further north.[45]

Around mid-October, when the Pleiades appear (a sign of fair weather and the time for sailing), the canoes set out from the islands. Yams, bananas and sweet potatoes that have been mixed with turtle fat, roasted, dried and placed in bamboo tubes are sealed and placed in the canoes. These are exchanged in a multitude of minor transactions for bird of paradise and cassowary feathers, dogs' teeth necklaces from *Op Deudai* (Papua New Guinea) and red and white ochre, emu feathers and emu leg bones (for digging sticks) from the island of Muri and *Keo Deudai* (Cape York). These expeditions were exceptionally dangerous and regarded as tests of strength. They moved from east to west, travelling leeward to Boigu, an island off *Op Deudai* (Papua New Guinea). This path from east to west is also the path taken by the stars; 'life mirrors the crescent-shaped path of the stars of *Tagai*, from springtime

---

44 Wells 1973:31–36.

45 Sharp 1993:6.

when *Seg* (Orion) and *Usiam* (the Pleiades) come up to the time of their decline.[46] Unfortunately, there are no details available about the navigation skills or voyaging star maps that were used by the Meriam people or other Torres Strait Islanders. It has been noted that what was required for voyaging was discernment which 'engages the senses in a unity which takes in "everything", as in "tracking" or "reading" the sea.'[47]

Fishing was an important activity among many Australian Aboriginal groups and when Arcturus (*Alpha Bootis*) appeared in the eastern sky, for example, many people knew it was time to make fish traps.[48]

The people of Groote Eylandt[49] and Yirrkala[50] in Arnhem Land had extensive knowledge about the relationship between tides and the waxing and waning of the moon. The people thought that when the tide was high, the water ran into the moon filling it up, making it fat and round. Conversely, when the tides were low, the water ran out of the moon, leaving it thin and small. When Charles Mountford, on one of his visits asked why the moon was still thin when the tides were high at new moon, it was explained to him that although only a small part of the moon was shining, like pearl shell, the dark body made fat by water flowing in from the high tide was present, but could not be seen.

For the Meriam people of the Torres Strait, the arrival of the wet season, *koki kerker*, in December signalled the time that fish could be caught in the stone fish-traps. Night was the time known in this partic-ular season for having low tides, when men could venture out the time known in this particular season for having low tides, when men could venture out after dark in six-crew canoes into the traps, assured in the knowledge that there were plenty of fish to spear. They used coconut-leaf torches made by binding together two long coconut branches. They

---

46 Sharp 1993:77.

47 Sharp 1993:78.

48 Bhathal and White (1991:9) do not specify the location of these groups.

49 Mountford 1956:484.

50 Mountford 1956:495–96.

speared the fish with bamboo-shafted and hardwood-pronged spears. A little later in the year, when the weather cooled and the winds turned around to the south, various varieties of sardine became available and were harvested in conical bamboo baskets. Shell fish were harvested at low tide from early April onwards.

Terrestrial Navigation

For a nomadic peoples, terrestrial spatial orientation and route finding are crucial skills and are usually very highly developed. David Lewis's investigations of land navigation among desert-dwelling Aborigines assured him that they show 'extraordinary activity of perception of natural signs and ability to interpret them, and almost total recall of every topographical feature of any country they had ever crossed'. Lewis travelled in the Western and Simpson Deserts over 7800 kilometres, 1000 kilometres of which was completely trackless terrain, accompanied by local Aboriginal men.[51]

In pre-contact times, people moved relatively frequently in particular areas over a certain range, the boundaries of which fluctuated.[52] Having travelled extensively with Aboriginal men, Lewis came to appreciate that the primary reference in physical orientation was the spiritual world, which manifested itself in terrestrial sacred sites and Dreaming tracks of the ancestors: the entire spiritual-physical world forms a coherent integrated whole. However, this highly developed spatial orientation capacity, relying on the emotionally charged spiritual and temporal aspects of the environment, he found to be primarily, a

---

51 1976:271. In 1972, Lewis travelled the Simpson Desert area with two Antikarinya (Andagarinja) men. In 1973, he travelled the Western Desert area, west of Papunya, with an Anmatjara man and a Pintupi man. In 1973, he travelled over much the same area as in 1973, but more extensively, and was accompanied by thirteen Pintupi and two Loritja (Luritja) men.

52 Berndt 1958:89–91.

daytime phenomenon. By night, without firesticks or other lights to show up the terrain, the Aboriginal men, despite their familiarity with the area and having travelled over the same ground during that day, became extremely disoriented. They showed an 'inability to keep direction by the stars' and moreover, did not attempt to use stellar references to update or check their mental maps as evening fell.[53]

Travelling after dark produced tense anxiety in the Aboriginal men and they kept the windows of the vehicle tightly wound up to deny access to dingos (*devil-devil papas*). It appears that nocturnal travelling was only undertaken under circumstances of severe necessity and always with firesticks carried at the rear of the line, walkers taking great care not to impair their night vision and their consequent ability to 'read the ground'.

Lewis tempers his remarks about the men's inability to use the stars in nocturnal orientation by commenting that his informants agreed they could use stars to guide them, if necessary, in a strange country at night. One man pointed to Orion as a potential guide, another pointed to Venus. Maegraith, in his survey of star lore of the Aranda and Luritja peoples of the Central Desert suggests that the Aboriginal people at the Hermannsberg Lutheran Mission in 1932 showed a distinct 'dislike of moving about after dark',[54] and that the difficulty he had in obtaining volunteers to help with his astronomical investigations, (they refused to rise in the early hours of the morning) was due, in part, to their fear of the dark.[55] Their detailed star knowledge had been gained by watching the stars from the shelter of the camp. Maegraith goes so far as to assert that 'no Central Australian native can find his [sic] way by night by reference to the stars, although in the daytime he [sic] possesses the utmost skill in respect of location'.[56]

Nonie Sharp, in her extensive study of the Meriam people, notes that despite the cultural significance and depth of their star knowledge, 'in

---

53 Lewis 1976:273–74.

54 Maegraith 1932:23.

55 Maegraith 1932:21–25.

56 Maegraith 1932:25.

each Islander household a lamp burned at night to ward off the powers of evil'.[57] Among the Yolngu[58] of Yirrkala in Arnhem Land, night was also perceived as a time of potential harm. People there need protection from *Galka* (sorcery), which is at its most powerful at night time. Ralph Piddington, an early anthropologist, writing of the Karadjeri people of Western Australia, implies that these Aborigines were also reluctant to venture out in the early hours of the morning. He says that the Karadjeri 'think of the various stars in terms of the time of year at which they are clearly visible ... during the early part of the night ... apparently this is the time of the night which is most important to them'.[59]

In many places throughout the country, it seems that Aboriginal people believed there were spirits abroad and their intentions were to injure or kill those who travelled alone, particularly at night.[60] In the Central and Western Desert areas, for example, there was reputed to be a large spirit dingo, *mamu*, who captured and ate the spirits of children who wandered. Sometimes the *mamu* succeeds in catching one of these little spirits as a meal for itself and its ghoulish companions. Should this happen, a child bereft of its *kuran* (spirit) would be expected to be listless and out of sorts the following morning. Only a traditional healer could control these dangerous night spirits.[61] In Arnhem Land, spirit people who have barbed spines growing from their elbows and knees, *nadubi*, could creep up on a solitary traveller and propel a spine into his or her body. On Groote Eylandt, dreaded spirits, *gurumukas*, are particularly active on dark nights and an Aboriginal person, if alone, risks being bitten on the back of the neck by the *gurumuka's* long projecting teeth. *Gurumukas*, however, are thought to avoid the light of campfires and Aboriginal people walking in groups.[62]

---

57 Maegraith 1993:XIII.

58 Reid 1986:61.

59 Maegraith 1932:394–95.

60 Roberts and Mountford 1974:168.

61 Mountford 1948:51 cf. Lewis 1976:274.

62 Roberts and Mountford 1974:168.

Mathews, however, suggests that the evening chilliness rather than the darkness as such was a relevant consideration among Aboriginal people moving around at night. On frosty winter nights, Aboriginal people that he observed around New South Wales and Victoria tended to stir in the early hours, about three or four hours before sunrise. 'The people have had their first sleep, and the cold begins to make itself felt. The men and women, especially those who are old, sit up and replenish their fires. While doing this, their attention is naturally directed to the sky.' [63] Among the Ngeumba people for example, in the cold mid-winter nights when the Pleiades rose about 3 or 4 am, Mathews reports that the old men took glowing coals and threw them from bark shovels up towards the spirit-women whom the stars represented, so that they (the Pleiades-women) would not make the morning too cold. Ngeumba women, moreover, were forbidden to look at the winter Pleiades because such an act was thought to increase the severity of the frost. If they broke this taboo, the women's eyes became bleary and they risked suffering uterine troubles.[64]

Yet when faced with dire necessity, fears of differing kinds were dissipated. Revenge expeditions or execution parties for example, were usually carried out by small groups of men 'usually at night and in operations which were well planned, based on good intelligence and timed to allow for the strike and return before dawn'.[65] There is also a reference by Dawson, a one-time Protector of Aborigines, to the importance of star knowledge among western Victorian groups for 'their night journeys'. Unfortunately, he does not elaborate upon the nature of these night journeys, but he does say that the constellation of Hydra was of 'great service to the aborigines in their night journeys, enabling them to judge the time of the night and the course to be taken in travelling'.[66]

---

63 Mathews 1905:78.
64 Mathews 1905:78–79.
65 Reynolds 1983:100.
66 Dawson 1981:101.

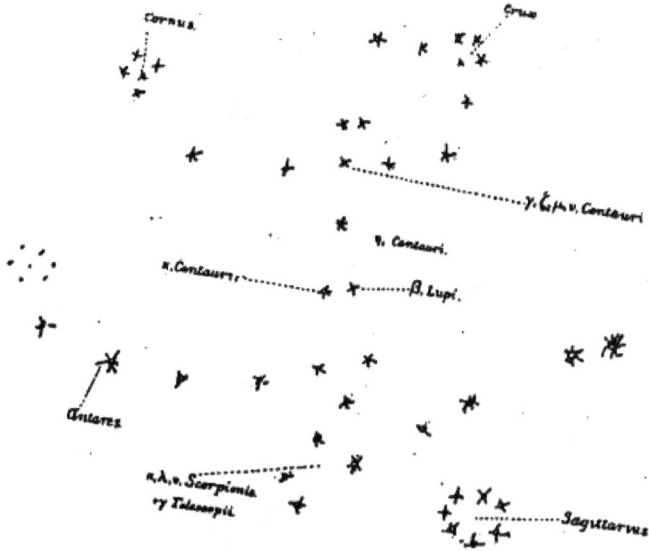

Drawing 1: The *Tagai* Constellation by Waria from Mabuiag (from Haddon, Cambridge University Press, 1912)

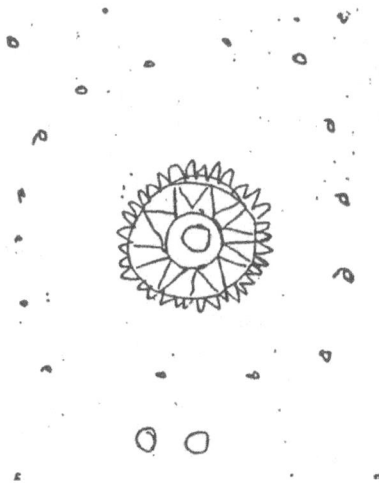

Drawing 2: *Kek* (Achernar) by Gizu from Mabuiag (from Haddon, Cambridge University Press, 1912)

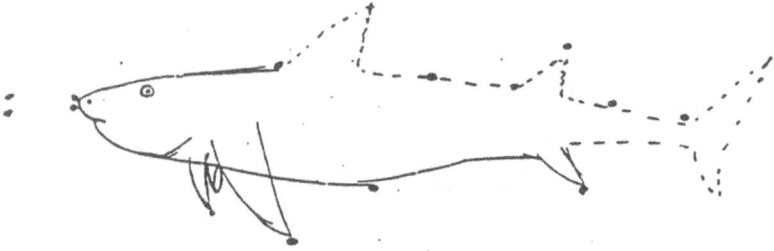

Drawing 3: The *Baidam* constellation by Naii from Mabuiag (from Haddon, Cambridge University Press, 1912)

Drawing 4: Drawings of constellations by Gizu from Mabuiag (from Haddon, Cambridge University Press, 1912)
A *Dogai wauralaig* or *I* (Altair)
B Dogai *kukilaig* or *Metakorab* (Vega)
C *Bu* (Delphinus)

Drawing 5: The *Tagai* Constellation by Mariget from Mabuiag (from Haddon, Cambridge University Press, 1912)

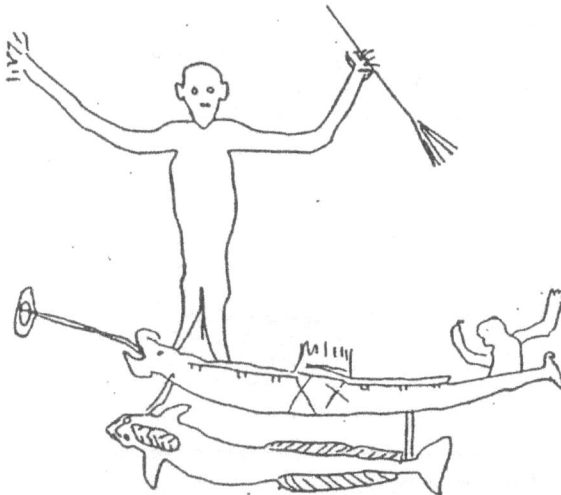

Drawing 6: *Tagai* and *Kareg* in their canoe by Gizu from Mabuiag (from Haddon, Cambridge University Press, 1912)

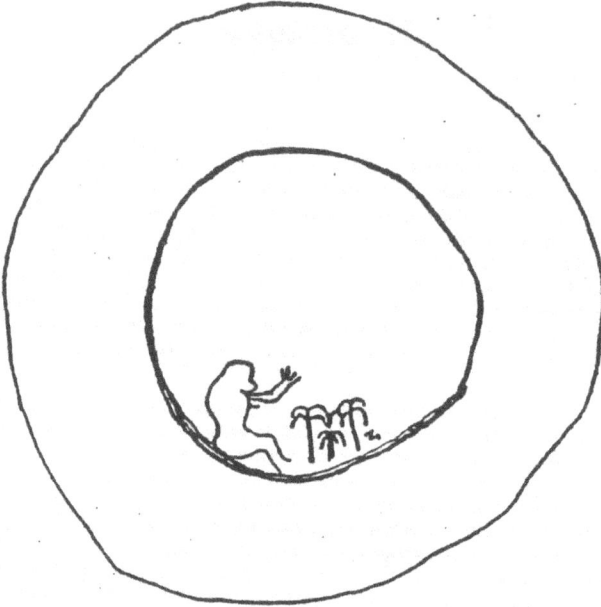

Drawing 7: The Moon with a halo, *Kubuwai,* by Gizu from Mabuiag (from Haddon, Cambridge University Press, 1912)

4

Mythology

Star lore held an important place in Aboriginal mythology, philosophy, history, religion and metaphysics over all parts of the country. Myths or traditional narratives were often associated with the stars and planets, the night sky being but one aspect of the natural environment, just one stage in the ongoing theatre of mythological drama. The projection of belief and symbol onto parts of the natural environment and the subsequent investment of spiritual status in them is a significant and underlying plank of Aboriginal and Torres Strait Islander societies. In the words of W.E.H. Stanner, 'most of the choir and furniture of heaven and earth are recognised by Aborigines as a vast sign-system ... [the Aboriginal person] moves, not in a landscape, but in a humanised realm saturated with significations.'[1]

The particular myths of a group of people are part of a much greater oral literary tradition. Together, they represent a vast and dramatic panorama of energies which underpin and inform the chaos and variety of human experience, describing, sourcing and powering it and its connection with other life forms and matter. These fantastic and ongoing mythical dramas also describe the limitations on and within human experience.[2] They address the human condition: the human experience of simply 'being' in its universality as well as in its particular cultural context. They can, in certain instances, allude to and elaborate historical events in the past, offer a charter to foster socially valued behaviour and bring into societal consciousness the shared dreams and fantasies of individual and collective psyches.

Individual narratives, then, were part of a cultural whole, part of the ongoing story of a group of people. They were often told or enacted in

1 Stanner 1965:227.

2 'The maggots at the centre' according to the Murinbata people in the Port Keats region of the Northern Territory (Stanner 1959:63–25).

a particular order, at a particular time in a person's life, in a particular season, in a particular setting, in a particular way. Some of the myths were known only to initiated men, or only to women. More often, they were known by all the adults within a community[3] and children in many instances were well acquainted with at least the outline of the stories. A relatively simple story that was told to a child, for example, was given a more detailed and embellished rendering when told to an adult, taking into account metaphor, contradiction and paradox. Esoteric significance was not readily revealed because it was frequently linked with sacred ritual and ceremonial practices.

The night sky was not an unusual topic in narratives or myth cycles. It was an extension or specific elaboration of the landscape, deemed especially significant in places because many of the creative ancestral beings, having performed or enacted their dramas on earth, had withdrawn to the sky and were believed to be eternally represented there. However, sky-residing ancestral beings were intrinsically linked to earthly forms and vice versa.

Many of the narratives recorded actual events or activities, large and small, routine and extraordinary. Each area, clan and language group had its own, albeit interconnected, sets or cycles of narratives, each with its own songs, dances, rituals, art and decoration. So the stories that have survived and made their way into modern literary forms are but a few, not unlike fragmentary parchment papers long dispersed from ancient texts. They are parts of larger narrative cycles that sought not only to describe and record, but also to inspire, torment and comfort. They gave meaning, passion and significance to each and every life and life-form. They acted as analogy, parable and metaphor, their symbolic meanings changing, re-charging and re-forming with different contexts and settings. According to American cosmologist Harrison,

> myths come to us as a legacy of priceless gems prized from their cosmic settings. Usually a myth has been recut and re-mounted more than once in the course of time. A full understanding of myth requires the reconstruction of the universe

---

3 Berndt and Berndt 1974:8.

in which it originated, even of the intermediate universes that modified and transmitted it, and an accurate interpretation is rarely if ever possible.[4]

Myths, like the people who inhabit them, also belonged to the environment or country from which they came. David Lewis describes how he became aware of this: 'Travelling with Loritja (Luritja) in their own country ... practically every place had its Dreaming, its story, its associated subsections and appropriate ceremonials. Most rock formations and waters were stations on long mythological tracks. With Wintinna Mick in the Simpson Desert the position differed only in that his people had migrated eastward comparatively recently into what was, properly speaking, Aranda and Arabana country. He was reluctant to tell me the myths, and I find his choice of words revealing: I am Antikarinya.[5] The stories belong to the Aranda and Arabana *country* (Lewis' emphasis). In other words, the myths were an integral part of the landscape itself'.[6]

Interpretation of myths or traditional narratives has been divided into four separate, although not necessarily incompatible or discrete categories by Australian anthropologist, Lester Hiatt.[7] He suggests that myth can be viewed at least in part, as a kind of history, or charter, or dream, or as ontology. Indeed, a myth may encompass more than one of these categories, embracing two or even three interpretive ideas.

Myth as Charter

A myth acting as a charter puts out time-honoured notions as a guide to culturally and socially appropriate behaviour. Narratives in this tradition are seen as constituting 'a conservative, socialising force whose

4 Harrison 1985:37.

5 Also 'Andagarinja'.

6 Lewis 1976:276–77.

7 Hiatt has reservations about the suggested categories' ability to comprehensively deal with all modern attempts to interpret the Australian material (1975:16–17, 20).

function is to sanctify existing institutions and to foster the values of sociality. They invest the social order with necessity by linking it caus- ally to an apocryphal past.[8] Nonie Sharp (1993) follows this tradition with her explanation of the vast constellation of the *Tagai*. The role of *Tagai* is to act as a source of instruction for the Meriam people. *Tagai*, a sea hero, represents a charter: 'I cannot walk the path that is *Usiam's* (the Pleiades) nor can I walk the path that is Seg's (Orion)'[9] ... 'for I must follow *teter mek*, the footprints made by my ancestors'.[10] The Meriam people take this to mean that stars have their own course in the heavens, that is, each star has its own journey to make: everything has a place in the world and its own path to follow. This charter entreats the Meriam to follow their own cultural traditions that they inherited from their forebears and to pass them on, intact, in due course. As a corollary, they must not encroach on that which does not belong to them. It is a belief that attributes to each creature, a destiny or province in the cosmos, a time and a place. Accompanying this charter is a cycle of myths and rit- uals which centre around *Malo-Bomai*, two significant culture heroes of the Meriam people. The celebration of ritual cycles in tune with natural cycles assures the accretion of human wisdom, envisaged as moving like a loosely coiled spiral and resembling the pattern on a cone shell.

Myth as history

Myth as history sees the narratives as pertaining to real events of the past. Hiatt suggests that the past events represented in myths fall into three main categories; that of migration, social organisation and partic- ular happenings in nature.[11]

---

8 Hiatt 1975:5. The main exponents of this analytic framework in the Australian context are Warner (1937), Piddington (1950) and the Berndts in their earlier publications (1951, 1964, 1970).

9 Lawrie 1937:373.

10 Sharp 1993:71.

11 Hiatt 1975:4. Spencer and Gillen (1899), Roheim (1925), Tindale

The anthropologist Norman Tindale has recorded a myth which refers to an eclipse which purportedly occurred in 1793.[12] In 1836, at the time of the first white settlement, the coastal groups in the Eyre Peninsula in South Australia were on the defensive against groups moving south, probably because of a scarcity in food resources. The pressures brought to bear by starving people were embodied in myth belonging to the Ngadjuri people which identified and expressed this stress in the form of an old cannibal woman and her two dogs, one red, one black, who collectively killed and ate people they encountered on their way south down the peninsula. In the myth, two jew lizard men were appointed to stand up to the old woman and her dogs. They did so by killing the three. But as a result, the sun which had never previously set, so the story goes, went down in the west, and to the dismay of the people, stayed down. One of the jew lizard men brought the sun back by (unsuccessfully at first), hurling boomerangs north, west, south and finally east. Tindale regards this as a possible description of an eclipse of the sun and his consultations with a former South Australian government astronomer, G.F. Dodwell, indicated that at that time, the most recent eclipse which had passed over Ngadjuri tribal lands had taken place on March 13, 1793, in the late afternoon.[13] 'It is possible,' concludes Tindale[14], 'that the story either touches on historical happenings of that date or was given a fresh setting at that time.'

The Australian historian, Henry Reynolds has reported a situation which occurred in the early nineteenth century around Adelaide and beyond, when the appearance of a comet[15] convinced South Australian Aborigines that powerful northern sorcerers were about to destroy the

---

(1938) and more recently Sutton (1988) are proponents of this interpretive tradition.

12 Tindale 1974:135.

13 Any earlier eclipses had occurred before 1600.

14 Tindale 1974:135.

15 It was probably the comet of 1811, which had a coma larger than the disc of the sun, as viewed from the earth.

town. The explorer, Edward Eyre commented at the time, that he was told the comet was 'the harbinger of all kinds of calamities, and more especially for white people. It was to overthrow Adelaide, destroy all the Europeans and their houses'.[16] This particular comet was seen as signalling the destruction of Adelaide because a senior man of one of the Aboriginal groups had been imprisoned in the local gaol. The narrative grew out of actual events.

Myth as Dream

Myth as dream sees the traditional narratives as shared fantasies attempting to rationalise the wish-fulfilment content of dreams.[17] An interesting version of this analytic view is discussed by the anthropologist Isobel White (1975) and concerns the open star cluster, the Pleiades. White asserts that in Central Australian myths the Pleiades are perceived as mythological women, variously described as the Seven or Many Sisters. They are invariably being chased by mythological men or a man. Their similarity to Greek mythology is worth noting, as the Pleiades were regarded as the seven daughters of old Atlas and Pleione. Their names were Alcyone *(Eta Tauri)*, Electra, Merope, Maia, Taygete, Celaeno, and Asterope. These seven sisters were constantly pursued by the hunter, Orion, and escaped by turning themselves into doves or rock-pigeons.[18]

---

16 In Reynolds 1983:89.

17 Hiatt 1985:7. These myths lend themselves to dream analysis, chiefly undertaken in the Australian context by Freudian-influenced anthropologists including Roheim (1925, 1945), Meggitt (1966) and Hiatt (1971). Roheim analysed myths from Central Australia and argued (1945) that myths about the Milky Way are concerned with projections of the so-called 'primal scene' (parental coitus) onto the night sky. The struggles in the stories are representations of separation and the ensuing anxiety this process necessarily entails (for males in Roheim's analysis).

18 Allen 1963:395. In China, the Pleiades were also seen as young

In Australian myths, much further afield than the Central Australian context, the women of the Pleiades are similarly pursued.[19] They spent much time running away from the unwelcome and usually illicit advances of a male (or males), who is (are) usually represented as the constellation of Orion, although there was some variation in precisely which celestial object was assigned the role of the assailant:

- Orion or certain stars in Orion[20]
- The moon (-man)[21]
- The Gemini twins Castor and Pollux (*Alpha and Beta Gemini*)[22]

women, the Seven Sisters of Industry, and were honoured particularly by girls.

19 In Arnhem Land, the men of Orion do not pursue the Pleiades women. The stars in Orion are three fishermen, with the Pleiades being seen as their wives. This is the case on Groote Island (Mountford 1956:482), in Millingimbi (Mountford 1956:493) and at Yirrkala (Mountford 1956:490–98).

20 Documented among the Wiilman in south-western Australia (Hassell 134:237); among the Ngadadjara people around Warburton in Western Australia (Tindale 1936:169–185; 1978:158–9); among the Anyamatana in northern South Australia (Mountford 1939:105, Roberts and Mountford 1974:74); among the Walbiri of Central Australia (Meggitt 1966:131–38); in western Central Australia (Mountford 1948:155, 167, 1976b:477–81); among Victorian groups generally (Smyth 1878:434), in particular, the Boorong of the Victorian mallee country (Stanbridge [1857] in MacPherson 1881:71), and the Wotjobaluk and Kulin (Massola 1968:108–9); among the Andagarinja at Yalata (Buckley et. al., 1968:113–24), at Indulkana (Buckley et. al., 1968:113), and at Ooldea (Berndt 19747–12); amongst the Pitjantjatjara people (Tindale 1936:176, Robinson 1966:91–93) and Anyamatana people in South Australia (Mountford 1939:105, Roberts and Mountford 1974:74), and at Cape Bedford in Queensland (Roth 1984 (5):8).

21 Documented on the east coast of New South Wales (Ridley 1875:145–6), Turbet 1989:123); among some east Arnhem Landers (Bozic and Marshall 1972:125–27) and at Ooldea in South Australia (Berndt and Berndt 1989:221–223).

22 Documented in the Western Desert (Mountford 1937:9).

- The Southern Cross (*Crux Australis*)[23]
- Aldebaran (*Alpha Tauri*)[24]
- The Morning Star[25]
- Canopus (*Alpha Carinae*)[26]
- an unspecified night sky residential ancestral hero.[27]

All these celestial objects, individual stars and constellations of stars, rise after the Pleiades, and follow their path across the night sky (see Diagram 3).

Amongst the Wongutha people originally from the eastern Goldfields region, subsequently Mount Margaret Mission in Western Australia, the Seven Sisters were pursued by men, one sister being temporarily caught, but it is unclear in the legend which star group represented the pursuers.[28] It was probably Orion given its prevalence as a pursuer in nearby areas.

White had the opportunity of observing the acting out of the Seven Sisters myths several times by Andagarinja women from Yalata and

---

23 Known as the Eaglehawk in the Kimberley region (Kaberry 1939:12).

24 Documented as being *Bunjellung* of the Clarence River of New South Wales (Mathews 1899:29, Mathews 1994:57); among the Kamilaroi of New South Wales (Peck 1933:215–224); among many Queensland groups (Peck 1933:215–224) and amongst the Wotjobaluk of Victoria (Massola 1968:108).

25 Documented as *Tjakamarra* among the Kukatja (Gugadja) people of the Kimberley (Green et al 1993:34–36; Berndt and Berndt 1989:281–282).

26 Known as *Waa* among western Victorian groups (Dawson 1981:100).

27 Documented among the Dieri (Howitt 1904:787) and among groups in New South Wales (Parker 1953:105–9, 125–7). His death in New South Wales was marked by the appearance of a meteorite (Parker 1953:113).

28 Groups who lived on the Great Sandy Desert in Western Australia also saw the Pleiades as women (*Jakulyukulyuwarnti*) but it is not clear that they are pursued (Lowe and Pike 1990:110). Among the Adnyamathanha (Adnyamatana) people of the Flinders Ranges, the Pleiades are also seen as a group of women (*Artunyi*), but it is also unclear whether they too are pursued by men (Tunbridge 1988:16). Amongst the Aranda and Luritja

Indulkana in South Australia. The myth was associated with the Seven Sisters ceremony and the celebration of a girl's first menstruation (*menarche*) performed by women for a girl during her seclusion away from the main camp. She was told a version of the story around a campfire by the designated 'boss' of the ceremony, who was also the acknowledged ritual leader of the women. Because she was older and past menopause, this woman took the part of the man in the performance of the Seven Sisters ceremony. In the version recited and mimed by the boss, *Njuru*, represented by the constellation of Orion, chased the seven women, the Pleiades, who came from the north-west. *Njuru* chased them across the (Western Australian) countryside, through Meekatharra, Wiluna, Laverton and Kalgoorlie to Cuneelee, where they went and hid in a cave to escape from him. However, *Njuru* caught one of the women (who it turned out, was his classificatory father's sister), and raped her. Because of the nature of this relationship, it was deemed an incestuous act and the woman subsequently became ill and died. The other six women continued on with *Njuru* in hot pursuit. When they stopped to camp at Anmanggu in the Musgrave Ranges, he stayed close by and became excited by the sight and smell of one of the women urinating. He sent his penis underground in order to rape her. Angered, the women set their dogs on to the penis. As a result, it is severed and becomes *Jula*, a separate entity.

This particular version of the myth extends from areas west of the Warburton Range in Western Australia, over the Rawlinson, Mann and Musgrave Ranges, reaching Glen Helen in Central Australia, in the country of the Western Aranda people.[29]

---

groups of central Australia, the Pleiades are also seen as a group of women associated with male circumcision ceremonies (Strehlow 1907:24). In addition, Mathews (1905:81) has recorded that along the Darling River in New South Wales, from Bourke to Louth, the Pleiades were also seen as a group of young women who went out in search of yams. A whirlwind came and carried them up into the sky. It is unclear if a man was in pursuit.

29 According to Mountford (1976b:462), 'at some point between the

In myths told by men and those told by both men and women, sexual relations consist of sexual conquest and submission including rape, incest, adultery and seduction, whereas in myths told by women, sexual intercourse, though less violently represented, is met with considerable resistance and a degree of ambivalence. White interprets these differences as symbolising 'the desires or fears of the dreamer[30]: the men's dreams are represented mythologically in violent and illicit sexual encounters, whereas the women's desires are shown as more ambivalent with sexual desire being accompanied by a fear of consequences.

White suggests that these myths, as dreams of wish-fulfilment, reflect the open as well as the covert hostility and antagonism between the sexes in a culture whose values are primarily male dominated. She suggests that the myths have the effect of rendering violent rape in the everyday lives of these people infrequent and unnecessary. Male dominance as a value is validated and reinforced by both men's and women's myths and rituals.

This analysis could be extended to cover many Australian groups as myths based on the Pleiades, as pursued women, form part of a much larger group of myths concerned with gender relations.

Myth as Ontology

Myth as ontology views narratives in conjunction with ritual and symbols as expressing ideas about the nature of reality and in particular, the human condition.[31] The views of anthropologist Kenneth Maddock (1975) about emu myths fall broadly into this perspective.

Petermann and Mann mythical route, the name of the man of Orion was changed from *Jula* to *Nirunja*, and that of the Seven Sisters from *Kunkarunkara* to *Kunkarangkalpa*'. From accounts by Tindale (1959 in Mountford 1976b:462), this particular version extends south to Ooldea and north to Haasts Bluff and Yuendumu.

30 White 1975:138.

31 Stanner (1959–63) based on the working assumptions of Eliade

The emu among many Aboriginal peoples presents a taxonomic problem: its inability to fly, despite its bird-like appearance and behaviour (feathers and egg-laying) makes it somewhat anomalous. Anomalies defy boundaries and present problems about meanings: about the nature of human as opposed to non-human; about 'us' as opposed to 'them'; about what constitutes and delineates 'other'. To explain the anomaly, many emu myths tell of injury and consequent diminution of the emu's power. Or the inversion of this, the enhancement of power by other birds having formerly been like the emu. As a result of the injury, often by being burnt, the emu escapes, sometimes to the sky and is represented there.[32]

In a myth told to Daisy Bates[33] probably at Ooldea, Emu (*Wej*) was married to Native Cat (*Jooteetch*) reputed to be a great hunter. One day while *Jooteetch* was out hunting, Wombat (*Wardu*) visited the camp and asked *Wej* to have sexual intercourse with him. *Wej* agreed to do so, but as dusk descended *Wej* entreated *Wardu* to leave. Before doing so, *Wardu* decorated *Wej* in red ochre. *Jooteetch* returned from a successful hunt and seeing *Wardu's* tracks asked *Wej*, where the ochre had come from. *Wej* initially lied, but eventually told her husband about the misdemeanour. *Jooteetch* ordered *Wej* to make a fire and when it was burning fiercely, he caught hold of her and threw her into it. But *Wej*,

---

(1960, 1973) and Lévi-Strauss (1966, 1967) are the main exponents of this analytical tradition in the Australian context.

32 Bhathal and White (1991:10) place an emu in the European constellation of Orion but the Aboriginal source of this equivalence is not documented. It probably refers to the account by Spencer and Gillen (1966:499) in which the Aranda are reported as seeing Orion as an emu. The Southern Cross is also represented as an emu among some groups, namely the Kulin and Ya-itma-thang of Victoria (Massola 1968:18) and the Yaoro from the Broome area in Western Australia (Durack 1969:238). Among the Wailwun of northern New South Wales, the emu is represented by the Coal Patch (Smyth 1982:286).

33 Ker Wilson 1977:50–60.

her arms burnt, escaped and flew up into the sky to become *Wej Mor*, the dark patch in the Milky Way.[34]

Another version of this myth is documented by Mountford,[35] in which Emu, *Waitch* is married to Wild Cat (*Chudic*). *Waitch* is seduced by *Coomal*, an Opossum. *Chudic* lights a fire to burn *Waitch* in retribution. But a strong wind created by the blaze of the fire sweeps *Waitch* up to the horns of the new moon. After a few nights the moon becomes so fat that it pushes the emu out. The stars whose task it is to hold up the sky-dome, agree to let *Waitch* camp near the Southern Cross if she will assist them in their task. *Waitch* spreads her wings to take her share of the weight. As a consequence, thunder is thought to be *Waitch*'s grumbling when her load is too heavy. On the occasions when she makes too much fuss, the sun-people create clouds filled with lightning and darken the sky, frightening *Waitch* until she quietens down. Because she is frequently frightened, she cries, her tears falling to the ground as rain. *Waitch* shares the task of supporting the world.

Maddock[35] has suggested that emu myths are frequently associated with fire and the vexed question concerning its correct possession and ownership. Emu myths attempt to resolve the emu's anomalous position by positing antagonism between the emu and a bird, implying that emus are associated more closely with birds who fly than with other creatures. Although flying and flightless birds belong to the same family, differences among them are akin to differences within a family. 'Differentiation usually is brought about by the emu's diminution'.[36] Categorisation and the casting of boundaries about the nature of reality is thus resolved through myth.

---

34 Which particular dark patch this might be is not further elaborated.

35 Maddock (1975:118) also notes that emu myths show a feminine emphasis among groups where the major transcendental power is seen as male (the All-Father) and a masculine emphasis in areas where the major transcendental power is female (the All-Mother).

36 Maddock 1975:119.

The Oral Tradition

There are many myths concerning the stars and the night sky in the rich, complex oral literature of Australian Aborigines and Torres Strait Islanders. This oral literature consists of narratives, tales, children's stories, song cycles, ritual chants, poems and more recently, short stories. Collectively, they demonstrate a great awareness and knowledge of the night sky and indicate the deep interconnectedness that the Australians had with it, as with other aspects of the natural environment. While there is a great deal of regional variation represented in this tradition, a few generalisations can be made.

The Milky Way

The Milky Way was significant to all groups of Aboriginal people across the country, and many artistic representations about it have been made (see Bark Paintings 1). It was most often represented as a celestial river.[37] How the celestial river was sourced or whether it led into its earthly counterparts is unclear. But there were exceptions.[38]

---

37 This is the case for Arnhem Land generally (Roberts and Mountford 1974:136, Maymuru 1978, Wells 1973:13–20, 1964:25–34), documented specifically on Groote Eylandt (Mountford 1956:479), at Oenpelli (Mountford 1956:487), at Millingimbi (Mountford 1956:491, 496–8); and at Murinbata (Worms 1946:121). It is also the case among North Queensland groups (Worms 1986:118) and Queensland, New South Wales and northern South Australian groups generally (Howitt 1904:432; Smyth 1972:286). It is also documented as being the situation among the Aranda and Luritja people of Central Australia (Maegraith 1932:19, Robinson 1966:84). It is noted specifically occurring among the Kamilaroi (or Euahlayi) (Parker 1905:95 in Mountford 1956:503); Murray River groups (Smyth 1878:434) and among western Victorian groups generally (Dawson 1931:99). Furthermore, the people of Central Australia, according to Mountford (1976b:450), saw the Milky Way as a creek 'with myriads of luminous stones on its surface'.

38 Elkin (1971 in Maddock 1975:112) notes that in some places across

Ritual practices were associated with the Milky Way, as among the Walbiri[39] in Central Australia. *Gadjari* rites involved a withdrawal from the company of women by the men, in order to perform ceremonies that re-enacted the original cutting up of the Milky Way by ancestor heroes to form the individual stars. The actors wore body decorations of white down to represent the stars. The initiation of young boys involved the manufacture from acacia wood of a number of slender bullroarers. From these, two were selected to form the basis of a string cross. The cross was soaked with arm-blood and, on completion, blood, charcoal and white down were used to decorate its surface with a star dreaming design. The initiate fixated on the string cross while he was being circumcised. It was believed that an old woman, having a relationship of mother's father's sister to the initiate, lived in the Milky Way. She kept watch over the initiate to ensure he came to no harm.[40]

---

the continent, the Milky Way is seen as sparks from fire, (the emu being associated with and frequently originally owning fire); it is also seen as the great creative spirit, the Rainbow Spirit in the Northern Kimberleys (Worms 1986:96, 127), among the Karadjeri and among the people from Roper River (Worms 1986:129); it was seen as flying foxes by some (Roberts and Mountford 1974:323); as mythical men among the Tiwi (Roberts and Mountford 1974:70) and as a large mythical canoe among the Lower River Murray groups in South Australia (Berndt and Berndt 1977:203, Berndt and Berndt 1993:224, 227, 243). Around Encounter Bay in South Australia, the Milky Way was a 'row of huts' amongst which were heaps of ashes from which smoke ascended (Meyer 1916:12). The Djuan of Central Australia also saw it as smoke, but originating from the world campfire of a respected and well-loved ancestor (Ellis 1991:119–121).

39 Recorded by Meggitt (1966:126).

40 It is interesting to contrast these views with other culturally inspired views of the Milky Way. According to Jaki (1973), the ancient Egyptians as methodical store-keepers of grain, for example, saw it as the work of the goddess, Isis, who spread large quantities of wheat across the sky; the gold-loving Incas saw it as golden star dust; the Arctic Eskimos saw it as a snowy band; Far Orient fishermen saw it as a school of fish frightened by the hook of a new moon; the Great Lakes Indians saw it as a muddy creek stirred up by a swimming turtle; and the Polynesians saw it as a

The Pleiades

The Pleiades were distinguished by all Australian Aboriginal groups and were mostly represented as a group, usually seven in number, of related women. In the majority of stories they are eternally pursued by men variously represented by Orion, the Southern Cross, Castor and Pollux, the Gemini twins, the Moon, Aldebaran (*Alpha Tauri*), the Morning Star (Venus), or Canopus as elaborated and discussed previously.

In Arnhem Land and on Groote Eylandt, the Pleiades women were seen as partners of their fishermen-husbands, who are represented as stars in the constellation of Orion (see Bark Paintings 2 and 3). The Arnhem Land constellation of *Tjirulpun*, in which the fishermen figure so prominently, takes in the European constellations of Orion, the Hyades, the Pleiades and many of the bright stars north and south of these groups.[41]

The Seven Sisters myth traverses thousands of kilometres of country as several separate narratives. Hundreds of localities feature in great song cycles which are still maintained and performed regularly in the Central and Western deserts. One Seven Sisters Dreaming track for example, passes just north of Warburton in Western Australia, and another just southeast of the town. Catherine and Ronald Berndt insist that the Seven sisters is a 'basic section of a myth-story that is on the fringe of more complex religious affairs'[42] Versions of the story have been collected from a myriad of places covering the length and breadth of the continent. In most versions, the core motif is the pursuit of unwilling or at least ambivalent young women by a man or a pair of men (who may be two manifestations of the same man). The man (or men) catch up with one of more of the women and there ensue scenes

---

cloud-eating shark. Over and above these local representations, comments Jaki, it is generally seen as a Way or a Road, the symbol of a journey.

41 According to the Northern Hemisphere-oriented Mountford (1976b:460), 'this beautiful constellation covers the largest part of the winter [sic] sky'.

42 Berndt and Berndt1989:399.

of rape or attempted rape. The women finally escape into the sky and are transformed into the star cluster known as the Pleiades.

An interesting variant of the myth of the Pleiades as women pursued by a man or men is the narrative told by the Pirt kopan noot people of Western Victoria. According to this account, the Pleiades are the six attendants of a 'Queen' called *Gneeanggar* who is a wedge-tailed eagle represented by the star Sirius (*Alpha Canis Majorus*). Canopus (*Alpha Carinae*) is a crow called *Waa*, who fell in love with the majestic woman. She refused his advances. *Waa* did not give up. Hearing that the woman and her attendants were going in search of white grubs, *Waa* turned himself into a grub and hid in the stem of a tree. As the attendants thrust their hooks into the hole bored by *Waa* into the stem, Waa broke the hook-points. Then the woman thrust a bone hook into the hole and *Waa* allowed himself to be drawn out and assumed the form of a giant. He then ran off with her.[43]

In western New South Wales, the Seven Sisters (*the Meamis*) flee their male tormentor, *Wurrunuh*, and escape into the sky to become the Pleiades. Later the *Berai-berai*, the *Meamis'* lovers, follow the women into the sky, becoming the constellation of Orion.[44]

There are a few instances in Australia where the Pleiades were not seen as young women. As previously discussed, they were seen as (male) members of *Tagai's* disloyal crew on the islands of the Torres Strait. On Melville and Bathurst Islands, they were looked upon as a mob of kangaroos pursued by the stars of Orion, which were seen as a pack of dingoes.[45] They were viewed as a number of gum trees under which the spirits of the dead shelter on their way to their eternal resting place.[46] Among the Kuurn kopan noot and Mara peoples of western Victoria,

---

43 Dawson 1981:100. His use of the word 'Queen' is inappropriate in this particular context.

44 Parker 1953:105–109, 125–127.

45 Mountford 1976b:460.

46 Mountford (in Roberts and Mountford 1974:74) does not indicate the location of this notion.

the Pleiades are a flock of female cockatoos,[47] and among the Wailwun people of northern New South Wales, they are *worrul,* a bees' nest.[48]

The Seven Sisters star cluster is also regarded as a place of exile. In an Alawa myth from the Roper River area in the Northern Territory, a boy attempted to commit incest with his grandmother. When she refused, the boy bit his grandmother's clitoris. The grandfather banished both of them to 'the *gomerindji* constellation' (the Seven Sisters). The spirits of the woman and the boy entered the *gomerindji* constellation and remain there today, stuck together, the boy still biting his grandmother's clitoris.[49] The Seven Sisters are not always on the run from a man (or men)! [50] In western Arnhem Land, the men of Orion paddle their canoe along the sky river, the Milky Way, whilst their wives seated in the stern catch fish in its waters. In north-eastern Arnhem Land, whilst Orion represents a canoe-load of men, (*the Tjirulpun*), their wives, represented by the Pleiades, are seated in a separate canoe. Both groups, so the story goes, have caught many fish, but a heavy storm in the ancestral past swamped both canoes and all the occupants were drowned. The Aboriginal people of Groote Eylandt, however, view the main stars of

---

47 Dawson 1981:100; Massola 1968:18.

48 Smyth 1982:286.

49 Berndt and Berndt 1989:283–284.

50 There are instances in the stories where, for example, they make a barrier to stem flood waters (which subsequently form the Southern Ocean) caused when two brothers quarrel. One brother jabs the water-bag of the other, spreading water over the land, eventually drowning them both. Their spirits subsequently went to the sky to become two stars on the western side of the Milky Way (Berndt and Berndt 1989:44–45). The Seven Sisters are also responsible for circumcising the mythical ancestral being Nyirana and are thus associated with male circumcision ceremonies documented amongst the Adnyamathanha people of the Flinders Ranges (Tunbridge 1988:6) and the Aranda and Luritja groups of Central Australia (Strehlow 1907:23–4). Groups from around the Clarence River area of New South Wales saw the Seven Sisters as being exceptionally clever, owning special yamsticks (Buchanan 1992:73–74) with charms inserted to protect them from enemies (Mathews 1994:57).

Orion as the three fishermen (the *Burum-burum-runja*), the small stars nearby are their children, and the so-called 'sword' of Orion represents the fish that have been caught. The wives (the *Wutaringa* women) of the fishermen are the Pleiades, but they are believed to be resting in their hut.[51]

The Pleiades star cluster, in combination with other single stars and constellations, is clearly very significant throughout the country.

The Magellanic Clouds

The Magellanic Clouds were distinguished and named by most Aboriginal groups (see Bark Paintings 4). The Clouds, which are very prominent in southern night skies, are small galaxies in their own right and most frequently represent the camps of sky-people.[52]

Some Aboriginal groups saw them differently. Among the Karadjeri, they were seen as two snakes who represented two sky-heroes. Among some Victorian and New South Wales groups, the Large Magellanic Cloud was often represented as a short-nosed bandicoot, with the Small Magellanic Cloud being a kangaroo-rat.[53] They were seen as fish by the Lunga people of the Kimberley region,[54] as camps of the

---

51 Mountford 1976b:460.

52 This notion is documented as occurring on Groote Eylandt (Mountford 1956:484, Roberts and Mountford 1974:10), among the Aranda (Spencer and Gillen 1899:566, Mountford 1956:504) and in Western Desert areas (Mountford 194:156); in western New South Wales (Parker 1905:970) including the Njangomada (Worms 1986:134). However, among the southern Aranda, as well as being seen as the camps of two great men (nearby stars, known as 'two Gland-Poison Men' (Strehlow (1907) in Nilsson 1920:122), they are perceived as being endowed with evil, having the potential to choke people at night when asleep (Spencer and Gillen 1946:55).

53 Mathews 1905:79.

54 Kaberry 1939:12.

Eaglehawk by the Wolmeri also from the Kimberleys[55] and as spirits of the dead among the Kamilaroi in northern New South Wales.[56] In the Western Desert,[57] sky-heroes resided in the Clouds and dealt with the good and bad spirits of Aboriginal people. Among western Victorian groups, the Large Magellanic Cloud was seen as a gigantic crane, who was also regarded as a male companion; the Small Magellanic Cloud was a female companion.[58]

The Dark Patches (Dark Nebulosity)

The dark patches that lie along the Galactic Equator of the Milky Way are important in Aboriginal versions of the night sky. Whereas Europeans distinguish and name only one dark patch, the Coal Sack (or Soot-bag in earlier times) near the Southern Cross (*Crux Australis*), Australian Aboriginal groups distinguish and name quite a few of them. On Groote Eylandt, the Coal Sack was seen as a rock cod,[59] as a plum tree in Oenpelli[60] and as a string cross used in initiation ceremonies among the Walbiri[61] and Aranda/Luritja groups.[62] Among western Victorian groups, the Coal Sack was known as *torong*, a fabulous animal, said to live in waterholes and lakes and known by the name for a bunyip.[63] Among other western Victorian groups, the Coal Sack was seen as a waterhole surrounded by celestial ancestral heroes, who

55 Kaberry 1939:12.

56 Berndt and Berndt 1977:413.

57 According to Mountford 1948:168; 1976b:454–455.

58 Dawson 1981:99.

59 Mountford 1956:485–487.

60 Mountford 1956:487.

61 Meggitt 1966:128.

62 Strehlow 1907:29.

63 According to Dawson (1981:99), it was so like a horse, 'that the natives on first seeing a horse took it for a bunyip, and so would not venture near it.'

were represented by the large stars around it. They were said to have come from the southern end of the celestial river, The Milky Way. These ancestral heroes were reputed to chase the smaller stars into the great river, where they set about spearing them.[64]

The dark patches were seen as the home of a creative spirit among the people of the Western Kimberleys, as the home of an evil spirit who abducts the brolga dancer among the Mandalbingu people of Arnhem Land,[65] as a totem board among the Ngadadjara of South Australia,[66] as a bullroarer among the Lunga of the Kimberleys,[67] and as an emu among the Wailwun of northern New South Wales[68] and the Nyulnyul people from Beagle Bay in north-western Australia.[69]

The sun and moon

The sun was represented, with very few exceptions, as a woman amongst Aboriginal groups and she was usually envisaged as wandering across the sky spreading warmth and light (see Bark Paintings 5). So important was she, that all groups have myths about her origin and continuity (see Appendix 1). The exceptions to this view were held by the Needwonee people from Tasmania's Southwest and people from the Murrumbidgee River area,[70] both of whom saw the sun as being male.

The sun, however, was not everywhere perceived as the source of heat. According to Manning, an Aboriginal man of his aquaintance from New South Wales thought such a notion to be ridiculous: 'If the sun makes the warm weather come in summer-time, why does he not

---

64 Dawson 1981:99.

65 Rule and Goodman 1979:36–45.

66 Rule and Goodman 1979:36–45.

67 Kaberry 1939:12.

68 Smyth 1972:286.

69 Charles 1993.

70 Plomley 1966:118 and Peck 1933:55–64 respectively.

make the winter warm, for he is seen every day'? He believed that the influence which produces heat accompanies the Pleiades.[71]

The moon is nearly always a man and is frequently associated with death (or change of form and substance at death), menstruation and pregnancy (see Bark Paintings 6 and 7). As a consequence, staring at the moon is often deemed to be taboo, as for example, in the Mowanjum story about two boys being turned to stone[72] or being glued together[73] because they stared at the moon. There is also a story from Millingimbi about the moon's ability to kill if stared at,[74] and a report from Daisy Bates,[75] that if women looked at *Meeka*, the Moon Man, he would not give children to them.

There were more generalised taboos: in the tropical Bloomfield River area of Queensland for example, no-one was to stare at the moon for long because heavy rain was apt to fall. Children were forbidden to point at the moon with straight fingers, nor point to their own shadows in the moonlight, believing that these actions could bring death to their parents.[76] At Cape Bedford in Queensland, crabs caught at full moon were not considered good eating, a notion probably associated with the belief that at full moon, his belly was bloated and engorged after successful fishing expeditions.[77]

There were exceptions to the ascription of male gender to the moon.[78] Because its form changed regularly, it was occasionally seen as being female and pregnant.

---

71 Manning 1882:155.

72 Lucich 1969:33–34.

73 Utemorrah et al 1980:78.

74 Isaacs 1980:150.

75 In Isaacs 1980:150.

76 Roth 1984(5):7.

77 Roth 1984(5):7.

78 For the people of Tasmania's Southwest, the moon was *Vena* the wife of the sun (Plomley 1966:118). Among the Karruru people of the Nullabor

Aboriginal Constellations

Aboriginal constellations and their mythical representations do not match European constellations. Nor should one expect them to do so, as they arise directly from Aboriginal cultural life. Even the most recognised of the European constellations—Scorpius, the Southern Cross, Orion—rarely have a direct single equivalent. They are seen in combination with other star patterns and celestial phenomena, and are linked together by myth and narrative. Appendix 1[79] gives examples of stars and constellations, the outline of their associated mythical narratives and the many and varied places across the continent from which they come. It is worth noting that the myths and stories are taken out of their proper cycles and contexts, environmental and ritual, but they demonstrate the variety of star arrangements used. They translate

---

Plain the moon was also female:she was the wife of the Morning Star (Venus) and her mother-in-law was the Sun-woman (Isaacs 1980:49–51). Among the Jaralde (Yaraldi) of South Australia, the moon was a woman who became thin from so much coitus until she became pregnant and full every month (Berndt and Berndt 1993:232–3). The people around Encounter Bay in South Australia had a similar belief (Meyer 1846:11–12): 'She (the moon) stays a long time with the men, and from the effects of her intercourse with them, she becomes very thin, and wastes away to a mere skeleton ... She flies, and is secreted for some time, but is employed all the time in seeking roots which are so nourishing that in a short time she appears again, and fills out and becomes fat rapidly'. On the island of Mabuiag in the Torres Strait, the new moon is the 'tooth moon' and is unmarried; a little later she is termed 'young', then half-moon is married, next with child to full-moon, which is said to be 'big one married' (Ray in Haddon et al 1912 (4):225).

79 Appendix 1 is designed to show examples of the variety in pattern of celestial phenomena including the sun and the moon, used by Aboriginal people. It is not comprehensive in its coverage of myths and stars, and the Pleiades and the Milky Way are not included (except when they involve stories with other constellations) as they have already been discussed separately.

cultural heroes and heroines from their earthly context into the skies as was done by earlier inhabitants of Europe and Asia.

Wells has made an interesting observation about Aboriginal star narratives. She considers that they differ from other narratives in that star myths seem to divide into two categories.

> On the one hand, some stars represent wise persons who once lived on the earth and now live in the sky, from where they send messages of guidance and inspiration to the people on earth. On the other hand, the stars may represent people who have suffered defeat on earth, and have found refuge in the peaceful reaches of the heavens.[80]

A New Writing Tradition

As Australian Aboriginal people reassert their pride in and knowledge about their traditions, new forms are emerging. As well as recording their stories and traditions, some are writing histories, essays, poetry and short stories.

Modern short stories by the Aboriginal writer and painter, Sally Morgan, bring into a contemporary context the continuing fascination with celestial phenomenon, albeit post telescopes. 'Old Poker Face'[81] satirises the moon's association with mystery. Morgan sees the moon as a serious self-important old bore in contrast to the more cheerful, less obnoxious planets. In the story, blue/green planet Earth is created and, as its shadow passes over the moon's face, he is left with a grin. With each involuntary smile, the moon's mysteriousness is diminished, a great relief to the other celestial beings.

In 'The Night Sky',[82] Moonga, a young boy creates more light at night by dreaming that he can fly up to the cloud blanket and rip holes

---

80 Wells 1973:11.

81 Morgan 1992:8–10.

82 Morgan 1992:24–30.

in it. He manages to make stars! 'Gamin and Brush'[83] is the story of two child spirits who love to tease and play together. One day, they paint rings around Saturn. As a result, they are sent out to the cool blackness of outer space, where they meet a huge asteroid. The child spirits decide not to paint in spots, stripes, circles or rings, but in one colour. They choose red and splosh the bright red paint all over the huge asteroid. Once finished, they decide to move the huge red asteroid out of its orbit and present it as a gift to the Good Spirit. Just missing Saturn, the huge red asteroid collides with the Good Spirit. It explodes, leaving a small red core in orbit between Earth and Saturn and the Good Spirit covered in fine red powder. The red powder drifts towards Earth. Dusting himself off, the Good Spirit smiles, 'Mars' he says, pointing to the red core. 'The Red Centre of Australia,' he adds, pointing to the fine red powder on Earth.

Recent non-Aboriginal Writings on Aboriginal Astronomies

Three recent attempts to take account of Aboriginal astronomy have been made by Isaacs (1980), Bhathal and White (1991) and Haynes (1992). The possibility of star-mapping by indigenous Australians has been canvassed by Cairns (1993) and Cairns and Branagan (1992).

Isaacs presents a wide-ranging collection of Aboriginal myths, paying due respect to, and recognition of, the significance of the night sky in Aboriginal cultural life. She gives examples of narratives located around the sun, the moon, the planets Venus and Mars, and those major Aboriginal constellations which overlap with the most recognisable European ones, the Southern Cross, Orion, the Pleiades, Scorpius and the Milky Way. The myths that she has chosen display the great diversity of beliefs and cultural practices which characterise Australian astronomies.

---

83 Morgan 1992:37–42.

Bhathal and White give a short overview, 'Astronomy Dreaming' as a prelude to a white post-invasion history of scientific astronomy in Australia. In a brief summary, they recognise the astronomical knowledge of the Aboriginal people and its relation to myth, art, song and dance. The significance of varying seasonal activity signalled by the apparent movement of the stars is noted. Bhathal and White view the large body of myths associated with the night sky as simple charters used 'to transmit the morals of the society to the young, the night sky becoming a huge text book for the transmission of their oral culture'.[84] They conclude that Aboriginal astronomy is more concerned than modern scientific astronomy with social and moral relationships, and with practical observations 'for the survival of the tribe'.

In a more comprehensive account of Aboriginal astronomy, Haynes[85] concentrates on Aboriginal visual observations and their predictive and moral function in star lore and myth. She does not attempt to elucidate the cosmological underpinnings of Aboriginal astronomy, rather she seeks out equivalences.[86]

Her view is that Aboriginal observations

> were conducted not out of scientific curiosity—out of an interest in the stars for their own sake—but for essentially pragmatic reasons. Either they were an attempt to discover predictive correlations between the positions of the stars and other natural events important to the survival of the tribe ... or they provided a system of moral guidance and education in tribal lore—a function equally necessary to the continuation of the tribe's identity.[87]

---

84 Bhathal and White 1991:11.

85 Haynes relies substantially on the work of Maegraith (1932), Mountford (1956, 1958, 1976), Tindale (1974), Elkin (1964) and MacPherson (1881).

86 Using the same European celestial phenomena as Isaacs, substituting Mars with the Magellanic Clouds and adding meteors.

87 Haynes 1992:128–29.

This strictly functionalist view of Aboriginal astronomies and culture would seem to deny Aboriginal metaphysics, philosophy and aesthetics, all of which are informed by a sense of irony, imagination and humour. Aboriginal culture is a complex of imaginative interplays with and within the natural world, which is not to deny the significance for some purposes, of the predictive nature of Aboriginal astronomies.

Myth can be cast, received and interpreted in different ways and at many levels. It can act as allegory and as metaphor, so to see it simply as a set of cautionary tales, as moral charter, 'an illustrated textbook of morality and culture ... like the stained glass windows of medieval cathedrals'[88] tends to exclude the constellations of meanings in Aboriginal contexts. According to Stanner,

> these tales are neither simply illustrative nor simply explanatory, they are fanciful and poetic in content because they are based on visionary and intuitive insights into mysteries, and, if we are ever to understand them, we must always take them in their more complex context ... Aboriginal mythology is quite unlike Scandanavian, Indian, or Polynesian mythologies.[89]

Aboriginal thought and philosophy, like that of the European, were imbued with 'the metaphysical gift' capable of contemplation on the nature of being, and thus able to attempt to make sense of human experience and its condition on earth.[90]

---

88 Haynes 1992:129.

89 Stanner 1965;55.

90 Stanner 1956:55–56.

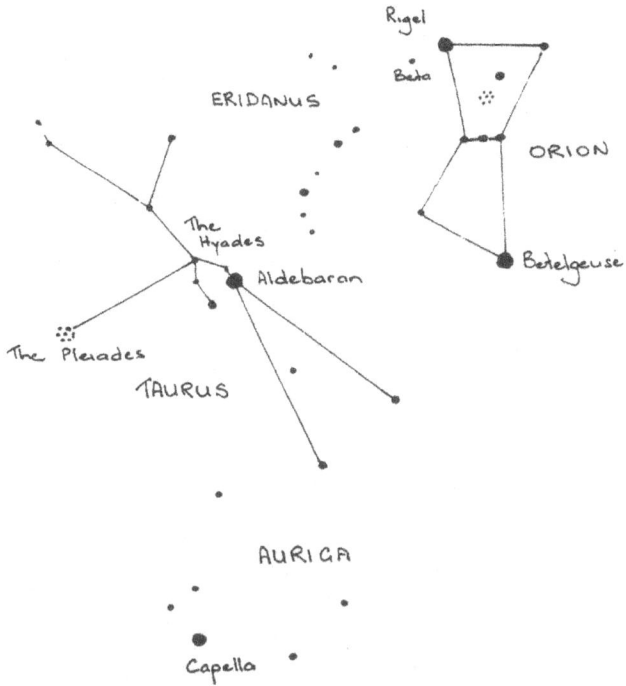

Diagram 1: Orion and Taurus

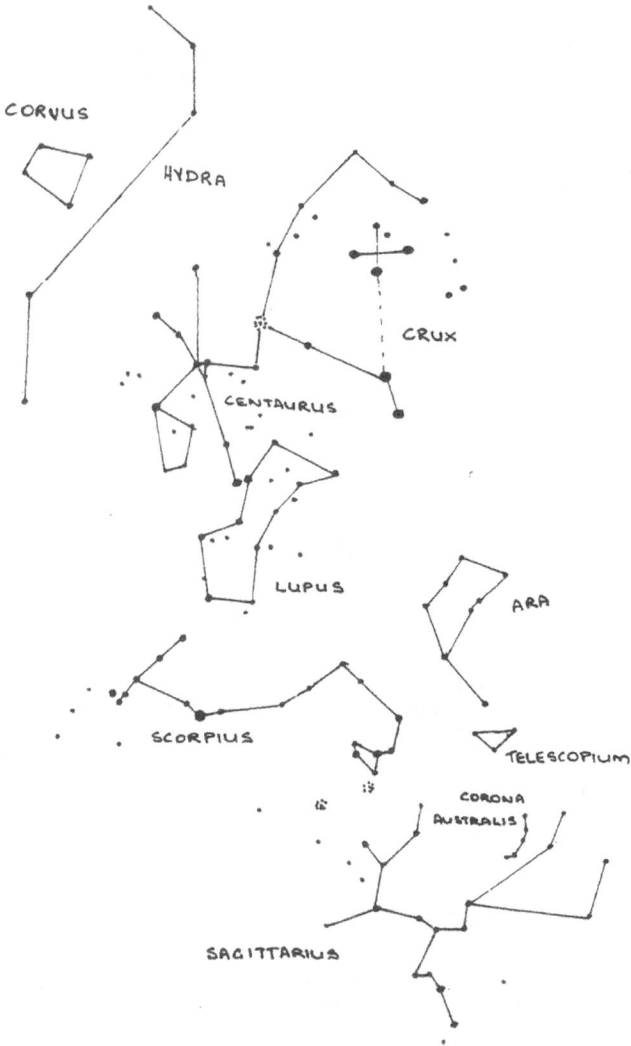

Diagram 2: Area of sky covered by the *Tagai*

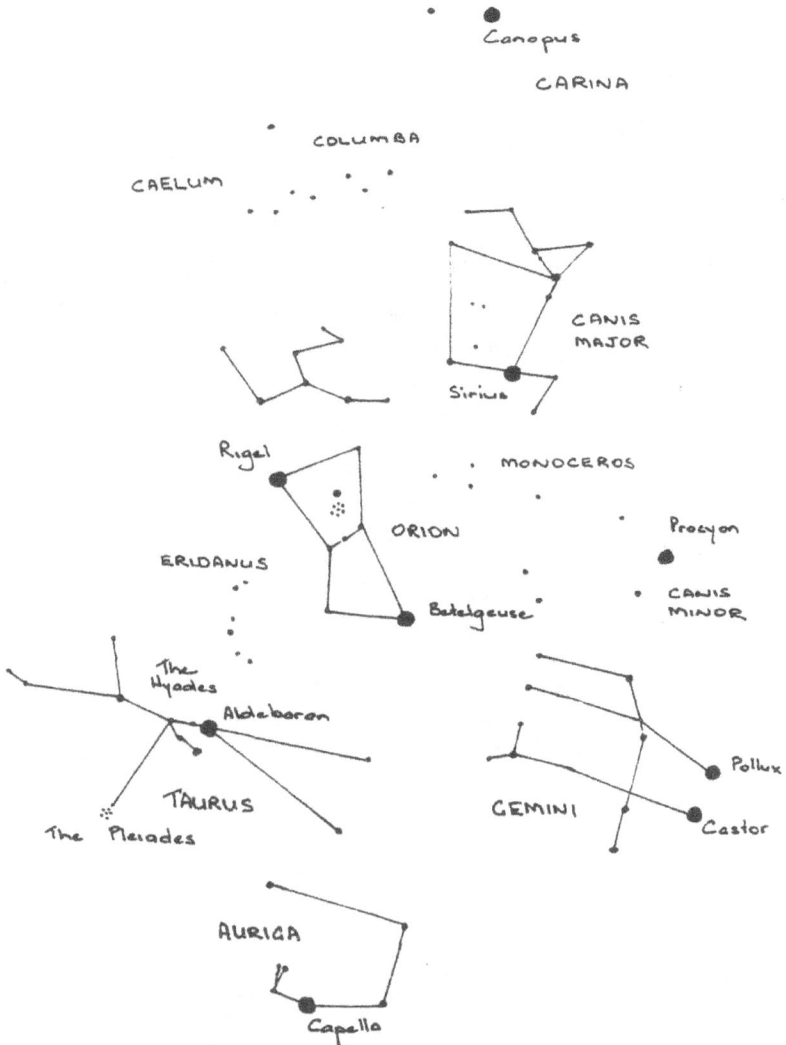

Diagram 3: Western Constellations involved in the Seven Sisters stories

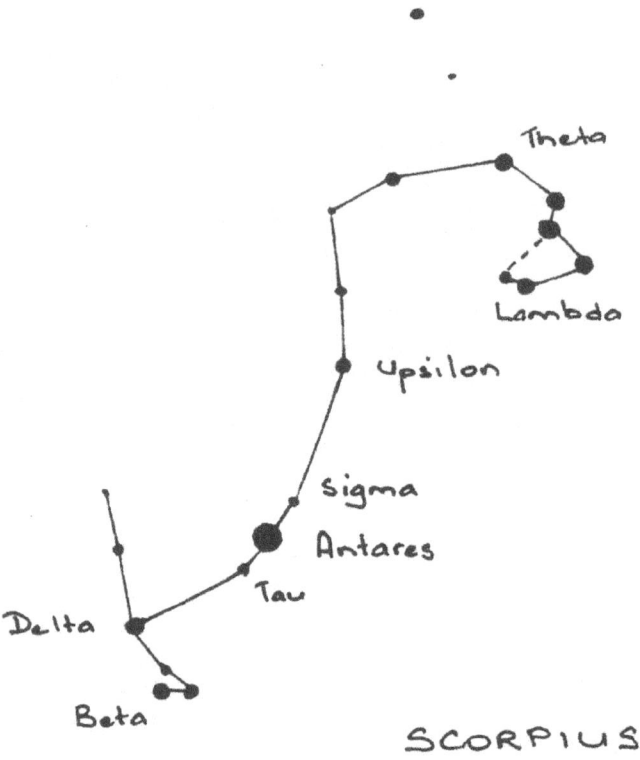

Diagram 4: Scorpius

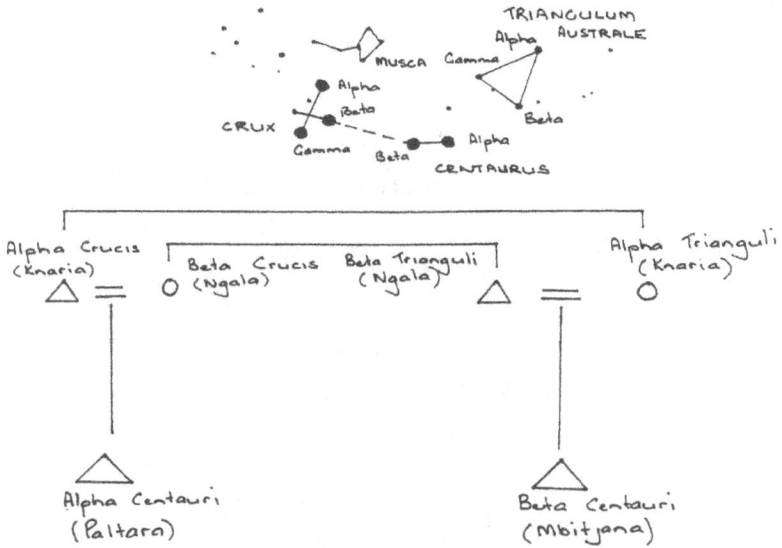

Diagram 5: Constellations and Kin Ties of Aranda/Luritja (N.T.) People

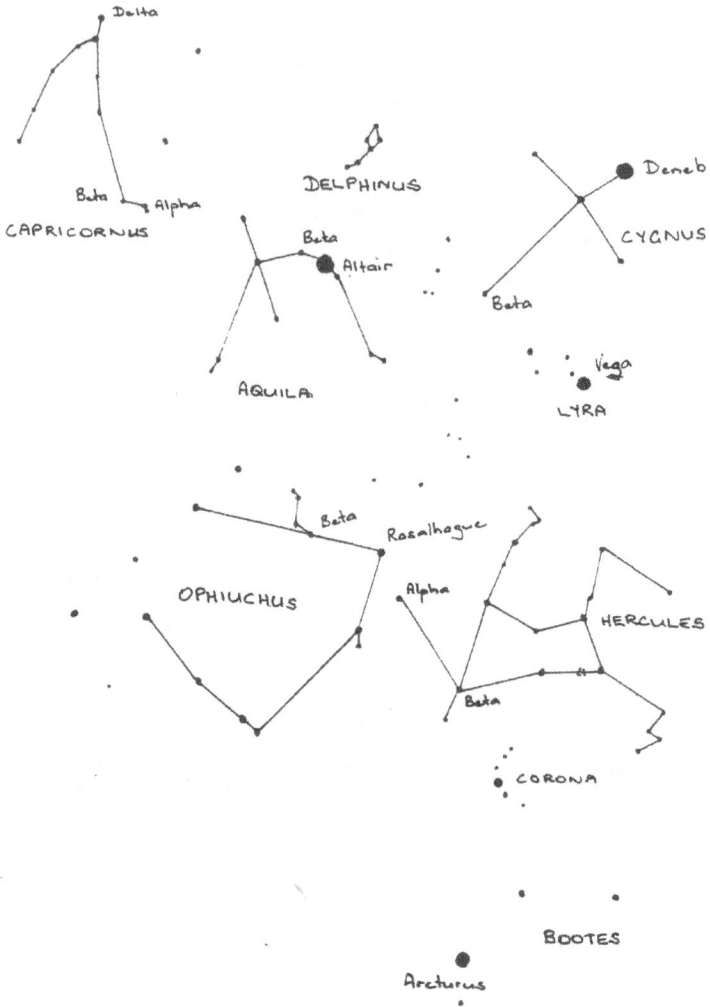

Diagram 6: Capricornus, Aquila, Cygnus, Lyra, Ophiuchus and Hercules

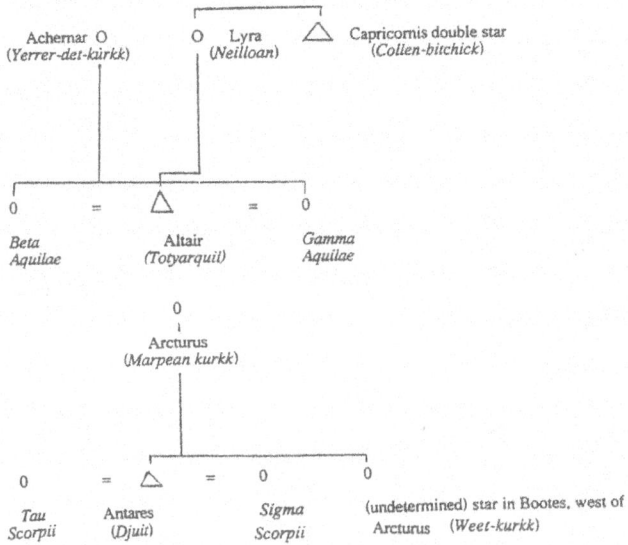

Diagram 7: Kin Ties represented by stars among the Booyong (Vic.) People

5

Social Relations and Kin Ties

Kinship classifications and relations were the cornerstone of Aboriginal societies: they formed the basis of social structure. Aboriginal people formally and systematically ordered their world, terrestrial and celestial, natural as well as cultural, into a number of discrete divisions or categories ('skins' in Aboriginal English), that regulated marriage as well as other activities. These categories were essentially social summaries of kinship relations.

In outline, five kinds of groupings occurred in Aboriginal societies. They are known to anthropologists as matrimoieties, patrimoieties, sections, semimoieties and subsections, dividing the Aboriginal cosmos into two, four, or eight divisions. No Aboriginal society is known to have had more than four (of the possible five) types of groupings. Matrimoieties and patrimoieties, the primary categories, divided the cosmos in two. Marriage arrangements were subject to these divisions, requiring that a man take his wife from the category to which he did not belong and vice versa. In other words, men and women of the same moiety (be it of patri- or matrilineal descent) could not marry. The particular moiety into which a child was born was determined by descent principles: patrimoiety referring to the father's group and matrimoiety referring to the mother's group.

Some societies for example, were bisected by matrimoieties and further divided by patrimoieties, cross-cutting the society into four equivalent segments, which then resembled the four categories of a section system. Categories ordered people, so that every man, woman and child belonged to one kind of category, and only to one. A person's category did not change, unlike kin relations, whose categories were relative for any individual; it was an absolute division of the cosmos. These systems applied in most places across the country, and their simplicity and generality made them particularly practical when relations and obligations between neighbours and strangers had to be deciphered. Even if the systems were different in kind, equivalences were possible to find, for different kinds were simply structural parts of a larger system, but they never replaced kinship relationships as the primary or ultimate tool for social interaction.[1] These systems lent themselves quite easily to the expansion of sociality. As well, they could be assigned symbolic roles that were connected to other species which had themselves been divided and classified.

One early observer commented that:

> Everything in nature, according to ... (Aboriginal people), is divided between the classes. The wind belongs to one and the rain belongs to the other. The sun is *Wutaroo*, and the moon is *Yungaroo*. The stars are divided between them; and, if a star is pointed out, they will tell you to which division it belongs.[2]

The great French sociologists, Emile Durkheim and Marcel Mauss[3], when discussing Aboriginal star lore go so far as to assert that the 'astrolological mythology of the Australians ... is moulded ... by the totemic organization.' They argue that because certain stars are particular ancestors and therefore belong to a moiety, a marriage category and a clan, then these particular stars are also classed in a given group, and assigned kin. They are thus accorded a definite place in society.

The night sky among groups and communities of Aboriginal and Torres Strait Islander people could be viewed, to some extent, as a mirror of social relations and structures on the ground: language groups, kin categories, 'classes' and their complex interrelationships were drawn on high. The sky heroes and heroines who resided in the sky, and who were represented by individual stars or groups of stars, planets, dark patches and upper atmospheric phenomena were in the long time past, and continued to be related to the people over whom they resided.

---

1 Maddock 1974:85.

2 According to Bridgman (Fison and Howitt 1880 in Maddock 1974:5) who observed the Aboriginal people of Port Mackay in Queensland.

3 In their classic work 'Primitive Classification' (1970:29).

The August night sky of the Aranda and Luritja people at Hermannsburg in Central Australia is a good example, as it has a relatively well-documented account of star groups and social relations and classes. Hermannsburg was settled by German-born Lutheran missionaries on the Finke River below Ntaria waterhole in the late 1870s. By 1929, when Maegraith visited and recorded their astronomy, both (Western) Aranda and Luritja people were living on the mission. The night sky at Hermannsburg was seen as two great camps separated by a large river, the Milky Way. All the stars to the east of the celestial river were known as Aranda camps and all the stars to the west of the river were seen as Luritja camps. Those stars which made up the Milky Way were thought to be a mixture of both Luritja and Aranda camps.

The Aranda and Luritja people, like most other Australian groups, had a system of categories or 'skin' groups which, among other activities, regulated and prescribed acceptable marriage liaisons. There were eight classes in the Aranda-Luritja system, however, only six were applied to the star camps and tracks.[4] These six of the eight classes were named *Knaria, Ngala, Paltara, Mbitjana, Panunga* and *Parula*.[5]

The two brightest stars of the Southern Cross, *Alpha* and *Beta Crucis* were thought to be the Luritja parents of *Alpha Centauri* (the upper Pointer). *Alpha Crucis* is a male belonging to the *Knaria* class. He is married to *Beta Crucis*, a woman who belongs to the *Ngala* class, and they have a son, *Alpha Centauri*, who is a *Paltara* boy. This combination of *Knaria-Ngala* parents with a male *Paltara* offspring strictly accords with the class system.[6] *Beta Centauri*, the other Pointer, is an Aranda man, the son of an Aranda father, *Alpha Trianguli* and mother, *Beta Trianguli*, who belong to the *Ngala* and *Knaria* classes respectively. *Beta Centauri* is a (cross) cousin of *Alpha Centauri* (*Paltara* class) and

---

4 In Maegraith's account.

5 Maegraith advances no explanation as to why only six are projected onto the night sky or conversely, why two (*Banata and Kamara*) are left out.

6 This also accords with Fry's findings (1931) in Strehlow 1947:174–175 when he analysed the Aranda marriage system.

belongs to the marriage class *Mbitjana*. Whereas the Luritja couple, *Alpha* and *Beta Crucis* and their offspring live in the west of the great creek *Ulbaia*, the Milky Way, the Aranda couple *Alpa* and *Beta Trianguli* and their son, *Beta Centari* live in the eastern section of the River (see Diagram 5).

The grouping of stars that Europeans know as the Southern Cross (*Crux Australis*) was not recognised as a meaningful pattern by either the Aranda or the Luritja peoples. Instead they have chosen the second and third magnitude stars *Gamma* and *Delta Crucis* along with the less prominent *Gamma* and *Delta Centauri* to form a constellation known as *Iritjiga*, the Eaglehawk. No particular star corresponds with any particular part of the hawk's anatomy, the constellation as a whole representing the bird.[7]

The constellation known to Europeans as Scorpius was of considerable importance to the Aranda and Luritja (see Diagram 4). It was almost vertically overhead when Maegraith carried out his investigations and made easy and clear viewing. The Aboriginal people divided it into two groups of stars, the stars in the head separated from those in the tail, to which were added some of the less bright stars of Sagittarius. *Lambda* and *Upsilon Scorpii* (near the end of the Scorpion's tail) were seen as the tracks of a *Panunga* man and a *Parula* woman respectively. They lay in the eastern section of the great celestial river and belonged to the Aranda group. *Iota* and *Kappa Scorpii* (in the bend of the Scorpion's tail) were the tracks of two *Panunga* men. The imaginary line that joins *Kappa Scorpii* with *Beta Sagittarii* in the east was seen as a spear and these stars were united in a dramatic myth. *Iota* and *Kappa Scorpii*, two Panunga men from the Aranda camp, are pursuing *Lambda Scorpii* (their classificatory brother and therefore also a *Panunga* man) and a woman, *Upsilon Scorpii*, whom *Lambda Scorpii* stole from *Iota Scorpii*. The spear belongs to the pursuers. The tracks of the escaping couple are represented by *Eta* and *Zeta Scorpii*. It is at this place in the star pattern that the couple were overtaken and killed vengefully by *Iota* and *Kappa Scorpii*. In the story, the brothers return with the bodies to their camp

---

7 Maegraith 1932:20–1.

and bury them in the creek *Ulbaia*, the Milky Way, digging the grave with a yam stick which is represented by the imaginary line joining *Theta Scorpii* and *Alpha Arae*.

Another narrative involves Antares (*Alpha Scorpii*) who was seen by the Aranda as *Arka* or 'tickly woman'. She was seen as flying west from the Aranda camp over the great celestial creek, to escape the attention of the men. She is fleeing with *Tau* and *Sigma Scorpii*, who accompany her on either side. They are also Aranda women, and belong to the *Mbitjana* class, whereas *Arka* belongs to the *Ngala* class. *Beta, Delta* and *Pi Scorpii* are seen as three Luritja sisters returning to the creek from a camp in the far west below the horizon. These women meet *Arka* as she flies westward, and she persuades them to turn back and return to their camp below the horizon. Antares, as well as being *Arka*, was described as 'the red ochre woman' (an obvious reference to its colour), who is proceeding from the creek with her digging stick towards a group of women in the west (the constellation known to Europeans as the Hyades), with whom she collects bush tucker and returns with it to the creek.

Altair (*Alpha Aquilae*) and Alshain (*Beta Aquilae*), the brightest stars in the constellation Europeans know as Aquila, the Eagle, represent the tracks of two brothers, pursuing an emu. The emu's tracks are represented by Vega (*Alpha Lyra*), *Eta* and *Pi Herculis*. The two brothers, one right-handed and the other left-handed, are from the Luritja group, and together they track and kill the emu at a place low down in the western sandhills. The other small stars in the European constellations of Aquila, Hercules, Lyra and Ophiuchus are the tracks of these two hunters and the emu. *Beta* and *Delta Cygni* are the tracks of a brother and an uncle (respectively) of the two Luritja hunters and, having followed the men at a distance, they assist in carrying the emu back to the celestial creek (see Diagram 6).

The star Arcturus (*Alpha Bootis*) is also named and is a *Panunga* man of the Luritja group. Other relevant stars in the August sky included Achernar (*Alpha Eridani*), seen as a large Aranda campfire around which men sit. The European constellation of Musca the Fly was seen as a mob of Aranda camps as were *Alpha Piscis, Alpha Pavonis,*

Alpha and *Beta Gruis.* Whatever the celestial phenomena, there existed the same definite, clear-cut division between the stars belonging to the two tribes, those in the east being invariably Aranda, those in the west invariably Luritja.

Although Maegraith did not see the summer constellations known to Europeans as the Hyades, the Pleiades in Taurus, or Orion, with his Aboriginal informants at Hermannsburg, they did describe to him the significance of some of the stars in these constellations. Aldebaran (*Alpha Tauri*), a red star, and the other Hyades are tracks of a party of young girls who are related to each other as cousins. Half of the cousins were *Mbitjana* and known as 'red', the other half were *Paltara* and called 'white'. They are arranged in two rows facing each other in a V-shape with Aldebaran being at the extremity of one arm of the V. The 'red' *Mbitjana* girls belong to the Aranda group and are the children of two other red stars, a *Ngala* man (probably *Alpha Tauri*) and a *Knaria* woman, a star not designated from the Aranda group. The 'white' Paltara girls' father is Venus, known as 'the daylight star' from the *Knaria* class, and their mother, a star not identified, is from the *Ngala* class. They also come from the Aranda group (see Diagram 1).

The Pleiades are the tracks of a group of young girls, considered to be 'not yet lubras' and assigned no class designation.[8] These young women live at a place known as *Intitakule,* now called Deep Well[9] or Kantala along Ellery Creek[10] and are associated with the coming of frost when the male circumcision ceremonies were held.[11] The European constellation of Orion consists of two groups, one being old *Ngala* men and the other old *Knaria* women.[12]

---

8 Neither Maegraith nor Spencer and Gillen (1899:00) who also refer to the Pleiades as young women, mention whether or not they are pursued by men, as they are in many other contexts across the continent.

9 Spencer and Gillen 1966:500.

10 Strehlow 1907:23.

11 Strehlow 1907:–4.

12 Spencer and Gillen report that among the Aranda at least, Orion was seen as an emu (1966:499).

For the Aranda people, the sun was regarded as being female and of the *Panunga* class. Myth has it that she came out of the earth as a spirit woman, at a place now marked by a large stone in the country of the Bandicoot people (*Quirra*) at *Ilparlinga*, some thirty miles north of Alice Springs. She was accompanied by her two *Panunga* sisters, the descendants of whom are still around. One of these women has undergone incarnation, choosing a *Panunga* mother, and is now *Ngala*.[13] Leaving these women at *Ilparlinga*, the sun ascended the sky and has done so every day since. The sisters remained in the country of the Bandicoot people, which gave rise to a totemic site for those who have a sun totem. Thus the sun is regarded as having a definite relationship to each individual member of the various groups. There is a ritual enacted by *Panunga*[14] which is associated with the two sisters left by the sun.

The Evening Star was a *Knaria*[15] woman who lived alone and was associated with a white stone which arose near a Gap in the MacDonnell Ranges known as Temple Bar, after she had left the earth. Every night, the Evening Star, known as *Ungamilia*, goes down to this stone. If an Aranda woman finds she has conceived a child when close to this place, the child will belong to the *Ungamilia* or Evening Star totem. There is a particular ritual associated with *Ungamilia* and is performed by certain *Knaria* men.

According to the well known Aboriginal Elder, Oodgeroo Noonuccal[16] each member of an Aboriginal group inherited at birth multiple totemic relationships (they could include conception, birth, 'cult' or ancestral affiliations, for example), implying a shared essence with a particular plant or animal of the region. They therefore became responsible for the ongoing welfare and continuity of that species. The word *oodgeroo*, for example, means paperbark tree. The bearer of this

---

13 Appungerta and Ungalla respectively in Spencer and Gillen's account (1966:496).

14 Panungra in Spencer and Gillen (1966:496).

15 Kumara in Spencer and Gillen (1966:496).

16 Noonuccal 1990:30.

particular totem would count the elegant saplings of the paperbark as part of his or her family. While individual plants and animals might well be used to serve human needs, a decline of the species reflects badly on its human relatives. The relationship between groups of humans and particular species of the natural world is one of stewardship. How these totemic beliefs are translated into protective practices in relation to stars is unclear.

There are other examples of social relations being represented in the night sky: among the Tiwi of Bathurst and Melville Islands, stars were thought to represent men and women. The reason they came to be in the sky involved social and kin relations on earth. One patrilineal clan of men from Melville Island, so the story goes, were constantly sneaking into the bush with the wives of other men, even though they had wives of their own. There was much jealousy and the ensuing fights resulted in several deaths. In order to escape retribution, the particular clan of men fled to the sky, creating the Milky Way. Because the stars in the Milky Way represent the male members of a clan, they are all thought to be related to one another. The women involved are represented as stars near the Milky Way, but they are dispersed from the main clan.[17]

There are many tantalising fragments about social relations and the night sky; among New South Wales and Victorian groups 'each star figuring in the myths belongs to a phratry, section, clan or other sub-division, precisely the same as the people of the tribe among whom the tale is current. The names of the subdivisions, as well as the names of the stars, change among the people inhabiting different parts of the coun-try'.[18] For the groups around the Clarence River in northern New South Wales, the Pleiades were a family of young women who all belonged to one particular tribal section known as *Wirrakan*, and Aldebaran (*Alpha Tauri*) was a man from another section called *Womboang*. Moreover, the arrangement of stars into meaningful patterns was based on the idea that 'a man and his wives, his family, his weapons, his dogs, are not generally far apart. Brothers, uncles and other relationships are often

17 Sims 1978:166.
18 Mathews 1905:79.

separated by considerable distances'.[19] The Pleiades in this area, were believed to send winter away as they disappeared in the western sky. Winter was meant to warn kinsmen on earth not to 'carry off a woman of the wrong totemic division, but to select wives in accordance with the tribal laws'.[20]

Along the Darling River area of New South Wales, the stars were divided between kinship classes so that the two large stars in the tail of the European Scorpion (probably *Lambda* and *Theta Scorpii*) belonged to the *Kilpungurra* division, as did the bright planet, Jupiter. A great hunter seen as Altair (*Alpha Aquilae*) belonged to the *Mukungurra* division as did Antares (*Alpha Scorpii*). 'Each clan or section of a tribe … (was) associated with an animal, a plant or a place, its totem'.[21] So *Alpha Crucis* (in the Southern Cross) along with kangaroos, fire, the non-stinking turtle, the plover and the laughing jackass were the totems of the *Pattyangal* (Pelican) clan of the Ngeumba people of western Victoria.

On Groote Eylandt, the Milky Way was seen as a sky river in whose waters were many large fish and waterlily bulbs. It was from this river that the star people gathered their food. All the stars in the section of the Milky Way west of an imaginary line between the European constellations of the Southern Cross (*Crux Australis*) and the Great Bear (*Ursa Major*) belonged to one moiety (*Wirinikapara*) and those to the east, belonged to another (*Oranikapara*).[22]

In the Kimberley region, the Lunga and Djaru people see the moon as belonging to the *djuru* subsection and as being central in a myth from the area that addresses the fact of death and the problem of wrong marriages.[23] The sun belongs to another subsection known as *nangala*.[24]

---

19 Mathews (1905:79) occasionally writes from a particularly male point of view.

20 Mathews 1899:28.

21 Mathews 1905:87.

22 Mountford 1956:481.

23 Marriages which do not conform to the kinship rules.

24 For the neighbouring Wolmeri people, the sun is of the *djuru*

The creation hero spirit, *Galalang* of the northern Kimberley groups is represented as living in the dark patch of the Milky Way, between the European constellations Centaurus and Scorpius. Remnants of his feathered headdress are seen in *Alpha* and *Beta Centauri* which also act as an 'allusion to *Galalang's* establishment of the two moieties within the tribe'.[25] In the eastern Kimberleys, the moon is regarded as a man of the *djanama* subsection. He has many wives represented by the dark patches on the moon's disc, all of whom are of the *nawala* subsection.[26]

Among the Walbiri people, the Milky Way is of enormous significance. It was seen as the source from which individual stars were created. Living in the Milky Way, there is an old woman who, during the painful male initiation rites involving circumcision, watches over the young boy who is being initiated. This old woman represented by an unnamed star, is believed to be related to the initiate, as his mother's father's sister.[27] The Milky Way itself was originally created by the sky heroes who were from a particular tribal section, the *Japaljarri-Jungarrayi* section, and who were associated with male initiation. The stars are seen to be associated only with this section and not with any other sections. Special sacred places on earth, so the story goes, fell out of the Milky. Way as shooting stars.[28]

To the Karruru people of the Nullabor Plain, the sun is a woman who is the mother of the morning star whose wife is the moon, thus introducing kin ties into the sky.[29] Kinship relations also link the stars of the people in the Victorian Mallee. Arcturus (*Alpha Bootis*) is the mother of Antares (*Alpha Scorpii*), and Vega (*Alpha Lyra*) is the mother of Altair (*Apha Aquilae*). Two small stars (or a double star) near the

---

subsection (Kaberry 1939:12–3).

25 Worms 1986:129.

26 Berndt and Berndt 1977:204.

27 Meggitt 1966:127.

28 Described in a painting on Door 29 at Yuendumu School by Paddy Japaljarri Sims (Warlukurlangu Artists 1987:127.

29 Isaacs 1980:51.

head of the European constellation Capricornus (probably *Gamma* and *Kappa Capricorni*) are the fingers of an uncle of Altair (*Alpha Aquilae*) and Achernar (*Alpha Eridani*) is the mother of Altair's wives (*Beta* and *Gamma Aquilae*)[30] (see Diagram 7). Among western Victorian groups, the stars and other celestial objects are all assigned a gender. Many of them are also married or related to one another. Sirius (*Alpha Canis Majoris*), for example, is the brother of the three stars in Orion's Belt (*Delta, Epsilon* and *Zeta Orionis*) who are related as sisters: he always follows them.[31]

In northwestern Arnhem Land, the moon is a man who belongs to the *Yiritja* moiety whereas the sun, a woman, belongs to the *Dua* moiety. They are married and their children are *Yiritja* as they follow the descent of their father, the moon. The sun is always in a hurry to get to her children for she can hear them crying, but she 'does not bring them over the world with her because she would kill all the *Dua* people'.[32] Likewise, the sky of the people of the western Central Desert region was divided into two. The stars in the winter constellations—Scorpius, Argo and Centaurus—belonged to the *nananduraka* group and the stars in the summer constellations—Orion, the Pleiades, and Eridanus —belonged to the *tanamildjan* group. The winds were similarly divided.[33]

In some parts of the country, there are constellations which are said to belong to certain clans or sections, and their constituent stars to individual people. On Murray Island in the Torres Strait for example, a constellation involving Vega and Altair is known as 'The Brothers'. When this constellation is rising, it belongs to one village and when it is setting, it belongs to another. Its name changes accordingly. Vega (*Narbet*) was said to be the property of a man who had inherited it from another, whilst Altair (*Keimer*) belonged to a man who had inherited

---

30 MacPherson 1881:4–75; Smyth 1972:433–34.

31 Dawson 1981:99–101.

32 Warner 1937:537–38.

33 Mountford 1976b.

from his father. These stars were also connected to certain identifiable stones, which were located on the land belonging to these men.[34]

Kinship for Aboriginal people was the dominant way of ordering their cosmos. And all aspects of the cosmos—whether it be people, plants, animals, winds or stars—were assigned a place in the system. All things were united, related and mutually dependent. Ideologically, at least, the system implied the well-being and continuity of all life forms by prescribing ways in which people were expected to relate and behave towards each other, as well as to other animate and inanimate life-forms. The stars were but part of this vast totemic network.

---

34 Rivers in Haddon 1912 (4):220.

6

Healing

Australian Aboriginal societies, like their Western equivalents, have evolved ideas and practices to deal with the reality of illness, injury and associated suffering. These ideas and practices were of course, embedded in the wider notions about the cosmos and the place of human beings in it.

Making Healers

Traditional Aboriginal healers were regarded as being wise, clever and being of 'high degree'. They could be male or female, although most were male. Their abilities and powers were very extensive and the processes by which a person became a healer were complex and differed between regions across the continent. However, there were common identifiable stages.[1]

Healers' powers were regarded as supernormal and usually supersensory. They were derived from two sources: ancestral heroes and spirits who were particularly adept in the art of healing, and previous healers who had links back to these ancestral spirits.[2] Thus, the making of healers involved contact with the ancestral spirits, many of whom resided in the sky-world. The rituals that healers underwent bestowed on them powers to pass through the confines of death, permitting them to visit the sky-country at will, travelling there on cords or strings, rainbows or shooting stars or via large trees and conversing with the residential ancestral heroes and spirits. Their association with the sky-country was thought to put healers in regular contact with star creatures and their lore.

1 See Elkin 1945; Berndt 1946–7; Reid 1986.
2 Elkin 1945:46.

Wuradjeri healers of western New South Wales could specialise in particular aspects of magic, in obtaining rain, for example, which required a particularly skilled and clever healer going unharmed through the dangers which accompanied a journey to the world beyond the sky where the water-bags were kept. When it was deemed necessary and advisable to obtain rain, a healer would be chosen and a particular time designated when he would undertake his skyward journey. On the auspicious night, he would 'sing' all the members of the camp into sound sleep. Sitting away from the camp, he would then sing the clouds down so that they were close to the ground. Next he would sing out his cord and send it vertically up towards the clouds and, lying on his back, his head curled towards his chest, his legs held up above the ground, he would sing himself up. Suspended like a spider, the cord would lift the healer upwards past the clouds. When he reached the sky-country, the healer let his cord gradually return to his body. He would stand up and look around.

> He could see the darkness of the night sky, and all the stars, which were the Ancestral Beings who had in the past climbed up here; being so close to them he could see their human forms, whereas from the earth they appeared merely as points of light of varying brilliance ... To pass into *Palima* (the place where the water-bags were kept), the doctor had to go through a fissure, through which the Ancestral Beings had passed when they left the earth. This fissure or cleft ... (had) two walls ... continually moving around ... On one side ... sat the Old Moon Man. He had a long beard which reached to his waist, while his penis was so long that he had to bring it up and wind it around his waist several times wearing it thus as a waist band. On the other side was the Sun Woman; she had protruding breasts, and sat in such a way that her large distended 'labia majora' revealed an extraordinary elongated clitoris, which covered the fire made by the sun and the daylight ... His (the healer's) actual journey was said to have taken no more than a few seconds.[3]

---

3 Berndt 1946–7:361–3.

Stars were instrumental in the making of healers in some instances, and were clearly associated with the activities of healers. In an initiation ceremony behind Mount Sugarloaf, near Lake Macquarie on coastal New South Wales, one of the healers presiding over a tooth evulsion ceremony was reported to have earlier been in the sky and had returned on a shooting star.[4]

Among the Wotjobaluk, Jupagalk, Mukjarawaint and Jajauring peoples of north-western Victoria, healers were made by a supernatural being known as *Ngatya*, who lived in the bush. *Ngatya* performed a ritual operation on the 'postulant' healer by inserting into the body magical objects such as quartz crystals. In these crystals, the powers of healing resided and when the operation was concluded, the wound was sealed without any scarring. Singing by the *Ngatya* took place and caused the 'postulant' to rise up. At the same time, it was believed, 'a star falls from the sky with the man's heart'.[5]

One particular supernatural creature associated with healers had a visible ancestor in the night sky. The ancestral spirit associated with Wuradjeri healers was a serpent-like creature known as *Wawi*. He lived in deep waterholes and made his den in mud banks. He could be contacted by healers who, having followed particular ritual practices, follow the rainbow after a rain shower to its end which rests over the waterhole.[6] One of *Wawi's* ancestors is believed to be the black streak in the Milky Way near the Southern Cross (*Crux Australis*)[7], known to Europeans as the Coal Sack.

Among the Anula people, a type of healer probably better understood as a sorcerer, was distinctly different from healers in other tribal groups. This particular profession was strictly hereditary, belonging exclusively to members of the Falling Star totem who were closely

---

4 Gunson 1974:51–3.

5 Elkin 1945:86.

6 Elkin 1945:100.

7 Mathews 1905:162.

associated with two unfriendly ancestral spirits living in the sky-world.[8] The powers of these people were concerned with evil-doing and sorcery, thereby distinguishing them from healers in most other Aboriginal groups.

The Healing Process

Healing procedures and rituals were many and varied among Aboriginal groups. A shooting star could act as a signal to the successful completion of a healing process, as indicated, for example, on the Wellesley Islands of the Gulf of Carpentaria. *Malgri* was a culturally specific illness found only on these islands. The treatment for it involved anybody and everybody in the vicinity. Initially, a fire was lit beside the prostrate victim. From the gathered crowd of people, the healer emerges. Kneeling beside the victim, he massages his own sweat into the victim's body. A grass or hair belt is unravelled to provide a long cord. One end of it is tied to the victim's foot while the other end is run down to the water, in order to point the way home for the intruding spirit. The healer commences the song of exorcism. Its innumerable verses are sung all through the night, while the assembled people eagerly scan the sky for a shooting star. The shooting star is regarded as the incarnation of *Malgri's* eye. It dives from the sky to indicate *Malgri's* dispossession and banishment. Once this has happened, the string is snapped and the victim recovers.[9]

Around the Bloomfield River area in Queensland, falling stars, known as *gi-we*, were associated with moving firesticks, and when a person fell ill far away from his or her home country, a lit firestick was thrown into the night sky in the direction of the sick person's country to the accompaniment of a cry telling the *gi-we* which tracks to take. The family of the ill person would hear the cry, see the message and know their kinsman or kinswoman was sick.[10]

---

8 Spencer and Gillen 1899:488–9.

9 Cawte 1974:110.

10 Roth 1984 (5):8.

In the Boulia district of Queensland, the moon was associated with healing. The people believed that, in the past, the earthworm healed the foot of an ancestral turkey by boring into its swollen flesh and sucking out the putrid matter. Every month the earthworm sends up one of his numerous brothers to remind people of his healing powers. Each moon, like their earthworm-brother, 'bores his way out of the ground, rises up on high, sinks once more and dies'.[11]

Bill Neidjie of the Gagadju people[12] describes the intimate connection which is thought to exist between the stars and the body:

Tree, grass, star ...

because star and tree working with you.

If you in city well I suppose lot of houses

You can't hardly look this star

but might be one night you look.

Have a look star because that's the feeling,

String, blood ... through your body.

That star just e working there ... see?

E working. I can see

Some of them small, you can't hardly see,

Always at night, if you lie down ...

look careful e working ... see?

When you sleep ... blood e pumping.

So you look ... e go pink, e come white.

See im work? E work.

In the night you dream, lay down,

That star e working for you.

Tree ... grass ...

---

11 Roth 1984 (5):7.

12 Neidjie 1989.

7

Astronomical Observations

Australian Aborigines and Torres Strait Islanders had, in traditional times at least, a deep appreciation of, and rich knowledge about, astronomy and astronomical events. The content of these astronomies is broad-ranging and indicates a great degree of regional diversity. It is therefore not possible to talk of an 'Aboriginal astronomy'. As previously discussed, the night sky Australia-wide shows great variation, not only in its seasonalities but also in its geographical latitudes which, south to north, vary to the extent of some 33 degrees.

Astronomical observation and enquiry were not a separate area of knowledge or endeavour reserved for the chosen few. Astronomy was an integral part of Aboriginal life and was reflected in their cultural life of storytelling, song, dance, art and ritual. It is not unreasonable to hypothesise that some Aboriginal societies, at least, took great pride in their knowledge of astronomy and their particular astronomical concepts. Members of the Boorong of the Victorian Mallee, for example, proudly proclaimed to William Stanbridge in 1857, that they were 'better acquainted with the stars than any other tribe'.[1] Indeed, Charles Mountford went so far as to assert that 'it would appear from my limited research that many Aborigines of the desert are aware of every star in their firmament, down to at least fourth magnitude, and most, if not all, of these stars would have myths associated with them'.[2]

The early surveyor Mathews noted that 'all Aboriginal tribes have names for many of the principal fixed stars, and also for remarkable stellar groups'.[3] He considered that because the stars near the ecliptic and the zenith change their positions in the night sky more rapidly than

---

1 In MacPherson 1881:79.

2 Mountford 1976b:449.

3 Mathews 1905:76.

those towards the poles, they more readily attract attention. Moreover, they could be more easily seen by people who camped in the then still thickly wooded country of Victoria and New South Wales. The horizon stars were barely visible in this context. Among the Wailwun in northern New South Wales, the star Phad (*Gamma Ursae Majoris*) and (probably) Merak (*Beta Ursae Majoris*), the only bright stars of Ursa Major[4] visible at that particular latitude, are known as *Ngung-gu*, 'white owls', for they are always low and move, as it were, 'under the branches of the high trees'.[5]

The moon's journey across the night sky is particularly important to Aboriginal people and is accompanied by numerous legends concerning the stars situated in the vicinity of its path. So Mathews considered that the Aborigines, at least groups in Victoria and New South Wales, had an equivalent of the zodiac.[6] The zodiac in the European cultural context is an imaginary belt of the night sky extending to seven degrees on each side of the ecliptic, within which are the apparent paths of the sun, moon and the principal planets. The orbits of the planets around the sun are in much the same plane. The orbital inclinations to the main plane of the solar system are 7° for Mercury, 3.5° for Venus, and less than 3° for Mars, Jupiter and Saturn. The European zodiac contains twelve constellations and hence twelve divisions or signs[7] remembered by the jingle:

> The Ram, the Bull, the Heavenly Twins,
>
> And next the Crab, the Lion shines,
>
> The Virgin and the Scales,
>
> The Scorpion, Archer, and the Goat,

---

4 Known variously as the Great Bear, the Plough or the Big Dipper.

5 Smyth 1972:286.

6 Mathews 1905:76.

7 It is worth noting that because of the precession of the equinoxes, each division now contains the constellation west of the one from which it originally took its name.

The man who holds the watering pot

And fish with glittering tails.[8]

The Aboriginal Australians could also give, with a fair degree of accuracy, the time of the heliacal rising of any star.[9] They clearly knew that stars rose in the east and moved across the sky to the west, as does the sun. They also knew of the more gradual annual shift of the star groups, and based complex seasonal and ritual calendars on the location of particular stars at dawn or dusk.

However, when assigning any particular star significance, it was not automatically because of brightness, an aspect on which Europeans tend to concentrate in making their constellations. For example, a star's position in relation to the Milky Way was significant to the Aranda and Luritja peoples. They also, as did other groups, assigned to stars a class and a kin category. Yet, among the Boorong, a star's relation lineally to the horizon was significant.[10]

The idea, as was prevalent in European astronomy, of joining the brighter points of light to form patterns had some equivalents, for example, the vast *Tagai* constellation of the Torres Strait (and extending into Papua), but it was by no means the only way Australian Aboriginal groups made sense of and took meaning from the night sky. Often a group of less luminous stars formed a meaningful pattern, for example, second- and third-magnitude stars *Gamma* and *Delta Crucis* along with the less prominent *Gamma* and *Delta Centauri* formed the irregular quadrangular arrangement in Aranda and Luritja astronomy. It was the constellation of the Eaglehawk, and no star corresponded to any particular part of its anatomy.[11]

The people of Groote Eylandt assigned significance to a relatively small and inconspicuous group of stars, while apparently disregarding nearby and much brighter first- and second-magnitude stars. This

---

8 Anon.

9 Piddington 1932:394.

10 MacPherson 1881.

11 Maegraith 1932:20.

constellation, *Unwala* (see Bark Paintings 9), is an unmarried spir-it-crab who lives by himself. He is represented by the curl of stars *Sigma, Delta, Rho, Zeta* and *Eta Hydrae*, having an average magnitude of 4.4.[12] Procyon (*Alpha Canis Minoris*) and Regulus (*Alpha Leonis*), two adjacent bright stars (with magnitudes of 0.36 and 1.35 respectively) are apparently disregarded.[13] Among the Boorong in Victoria, the bright stars Procyon, Spica, Regulus and Formalhaut go unmentioned in their astronomy, whereas much fainter stars are assigned significance.[14]

In some instances, much greater patterns were seen than was the case for Europeans. In the example of the *Tagai,* the Torres Strait Islands constellation, the European constellations of Sagittarius, Scorpius, Lupus, Centaurus, the Southern Cross, Corvus, part of Hydra and one star of Ara are all joined up to form the ancestral hero, *Tagai,* standing with his fishing spear and fruit in hand, in an anchored canoe. To that celestial picture are added the crewmen represented by the open star cluster of the Pleiades and three stars in the belt of Orion, who were thrown overboard in the narrative associated with the constellation[15] (see Diagram 2, Drawings 1, 5, 6). The large Arnhem land constellation of *Tjilpuna* (see Bark Paintings 9, Diagram 1) which tells the story of the three fishermen, takes in the European constellations of Orion, the Hyades, the Pleiades and most of the bright stars to the far north and far south of these groups. It covers the largest part of the wet season sky from December to March.[16]

Colour was also significant in the designation of stars as significant. The Aranda, for example, distinguish red, white, blue and yellow stars. Antares (*Alpha Scorpii*) is classified as *tataka indora* (very red) and the stars of the Hyades are divided into a line *tataka* (red) nearest

---

12 Haynes 1992:128.

13 Mountford 1956:479.

14 MacPherson 1881:41.

15 Sharp 1993:3–4.

16 Mountford 1956:493.

Aldebaran (*Alpha Tauri*), and a line of *tjilkera* (white).[17] The redness of Antares (*Alpha Scorpii*) is explained by this star being an ancestral woman who is decorated in red ochre.[18] The Gagadju also distinguish colour, for according to Bill Neidjie:[19]

> I see pink star
>
> I tell them 'That King Brown Snake'
>
> I see his eye ...
>
> that pink one.
>
> That star he work.
>
> He go pink, white, pink, white.
>
> That King Brown he look at night.

Aboriginal groups of the Darling River in Western New South Wales thought that the planet Jupiter[20] was once a man who lived on roast yams and went red because he spent so much time over the fire cooking his favourite food.[21] Among the Weilwun in northern New South Wales on the Barwon River at the junction of the Namoi, Arcturus (*Alpha Bootis*) was simply called *Guembila*, meaning 'red'.[22]

Aboriginal groups also knew that within a certain distance from the south celestial pole, stars never fall below the horizon. The Aranda and Luritja people claimed that their constellation of the Eaglehawk as well as *Alpha* and *Beta Centauri* were always visible, although sometimes they were high in the sky and sometimes they were low down.[23]

As well as patterns of stars, individual stars could also represent aspects of culture important to Aborigines across the country. Individually, they have been shown to represent a whole creature, a

---

17 Maegraith 1932:23.

18 Maegraith 1932:22.

19 Neidjie et al 1985:57.

20 It is more likely to be Mars.

21 Massola 1971:44–5.

22 Smyth 1972:286.

23 Maegraith 1932:24.

spirit ancestor, a possession, a place, a dwelling or a sacred site. Grouped together, as well as representing those objects already mentioned, in addition, they represented digging sticks, spears, canoes, tracks, campfires, tribal camps of related groups of people, animals, plants, food items and mythical ancestors. Moreover, qualities or states of being were signified. Among the Wailwun of northern New South Wales, for example, Canopus (*Alpha Carina*) was known as *Wumba*, meaning 'deaf', Venus was *Ngindigindoer*, meaning 'you are laughing', and Mars was known as *Gumba*, meaning 'fat'.[24] In addition, the perceived qualities of stars were assigned to ancestral beings. One manifestation of an ancestral being amongst western Arnhem Land people for example, was known as 'the running star'. He was pictured as a voracious creature who glowed and lapped up people with his long tongue.[25]

Yet, not only points or blurs of light were important in Aboriginal astronomies. The very dark patches between or beside the points and blurs of light were also distinguished, to a far greater extent than in European astronomy. On Groote Eylandt, for example, the European constellation of the Southern Cross (*Crux Australis*), the Pointers (*Alpha and Beta Centauri*) and the dark patch nearby known to Europeans as the Coal Sack, were seen as together forming a constellation (see Bark Paintings 8). The dark patch, as the story goes, was once a large fish which, while swimming in the waters of the celestial river was speared by *Alpha* and *Beta Crucis*, who were two brothers. The fish was dragged to the bank where the brothers divided it. They cooked their piece, each at his own fire, represented by *Delta* and *Gamma Crucis*. Nearby were two friends of the brothers, *Alpha* and *Beta Centauri*, who, at the time of the catch, had just returned from a hunt. They sat at their own campfire chanting whilst beating time with their boomerangs.[26] At Oenpelli, the Milky Way was similarly seen as a stream flowing across the sky. *Munguban*, the Coal Sack as Europeans know it, was seen as a large

---

24 Smyth 1972:286.

25 Berndt and Berndt 1989:25.

26 Mountford 1956:486.

plum tree (see Bark Paintings 8), which, during the wet season in late December, provided the celestial inhabitants with much fruit.[27]

It would also appear that in some regions at least, moving stars (the planets) were distinguished from the more fixed stars. Among the Western Desert people, Venus, Saturn and Jupiter, which were seen to be continually changing position with one another, were looked upon as two brothers and a dog. Venus, the elder brother (*Iruwanja*), was waited upon by the younger brother, Saturn (*Irukulpinja*), and their dog, Jupiter. Saturn and Jupiter spent most of their time catching food for Venus.[28] The movements of Mars were also noted by the Jaralde (Yaraldi) people in the lower Murray River area. Mars was seen to be a representation of an ancestral man and appeared to herald the spring (*riwuri*). As the ancestral man had eloped with the two wives of another ancestral man, he personified sexual activity and fertility.[29] The people of Mer (Murray Island) in the Torres Strait recognised planets as being different from stars because they identified them as not twinkling.[30]

Occurrences in nature were ascribed to particular sky phenomena at times. So, for example, among a Victorian group, survival of a particular species through a drought was attributed to a particular quirk in the constellation Europeans know as Coma Berenices, which was perceived as a tree with three large branches. At the junction of these branches was a small cavity which retained water despite the dry, parched earth all around. It was believed that birds drank at this tree cavity and were consequently sustained through the dry conditions.[31]

An interesting astronomy is displayed by the Boorong people of the Victorian mallee country. Based on observations made by William Stanbridge and reported to the Philosophical Institute of Victoria in September 1857, MacPherson suggests that the Boorong had developed

27 Mountford 1956:487.

28 Mountford 1976b:450.

29 Berndt and Berndt 1993:75–6.

30 Rivers (in Haddon 1912 (4):219.

31 Observed by Smyth (in Nilsson 1920:132).

a systematic grouping of their stars based on a lineal arrangement. Bright but isolated stars (that is, stars that do not conform to the particular lineal patterns) were not included in the groupings. Macpherson assuming that Stanbridge's observations were comprehensive, and placing the observations at the latitude where the Boorong lived at 36° S, located four significant linear groupings. These groupings were tolerably parallel to one another and to the horizon as they made their appearance in the eastern evening sky in their particular season. The lineal groupings that MacPherson distinguishes in Boorong astronomy consist of four triadic groups, each group representing three points in a line (at 36° S). Each of these triadic groups overlaps with one other group:

Group 1:   The three stars in Orion's belt - *Delta, Epsilon* and *Zeta Orionis*

The three stars in Scorpius, Antares in the middle and those either side - *Tau, Alpha* and *Sigma Scorpii*

The three stars in Aquila, Altair in the middle and those either side - *Beta, Alpha* and *Gamma Aquilae*

Group 2:   The triad in Orion's belt (above)

Aldebaran (*Alpha Tauri*)

The Pleiades

Group 3:   The triad in Scorpius around Antares (above)

Arcturus (*Alpha Bootis*)

Two stars in the head of the Scorpion's tail - probably *Iota* and *Kappa Scorpii*

Group 4:   Two stars near the head of Capricornus - probably *Delta* and *Gamma Capricornis* (or according to Smyth (1972: 434) a 'double star in the head of Capricornis'

Aquila triad (above)

Vega (Alpha Lyra)

Each of the four groups is associated with a separate mythic narrative, but they are interrelated.[32] In addition, the stars, like the ancestral

---

32 From information in Smyth 1972:433–4.

beings they represent, have intermarried (see diagram 7).

MacPherson regards the arrangement as

> 'an ingenious utilitarian scheme of the stars ... Necessity is
> the mother of invention, and no doubt the circumstances of
> aboriginal Herschels of the Mallee Scrub contributed to their
> success in the matter (of assisting observers in acquiring fa-
> cility in distinguishing the different stars).[33]

Certainly, the Boorong themselves were very proud of their system.

Unusual Events in the Night Sky

Unusual or unpredictable upper atmospheric events in the night sky
have been observed and interpreted by Aboriginal groups, although
records of these observations and interpretations are few and far
between. As keen and very astute observers of their natural environment, Aboriginal people were very familiar with the night sky and
unusual events were registered with curiosity and awe. However, one
commentator, Haynes, has asserted that Aboriginal astronomy was concerned with 'ongoing patterns of natural phenomena rather than with
extraordinary occurrences.'[34] Although recorded reactions to actual
unpredictable astronomical events are not prolific, nevertheless some
do exist. It is not possible to conclude that Aboriginal people were more
interested in one than the other.

Haynes finds their presumed greater interest in regular astronomical phenomena to be 'understandable since one of the main functions
of the mythology was to overcome the sense of helplessness otherwise
inevitable in a people so completely dependent for their survival upon
the natural world without technological means of controlling their
environment.'[35] Haynes unjustifiably attributes a sense of helplessness

---

33 MacPherson 1881:74–5.

34 Haynes 1992:139.

35 Haynes 1992:40

to Aborigines who lived within the framework of a traditionally based economy: there is no objective basis for doing so.[36]

---

36 Sahlins (1972) has advanced the idea that European notions of hunter/ gatherer societies, and in particular their economies - that they were meagre, and based on incessant and arduous labour - is an idea fuelled by a European bourgeois ethnocentrism based on a model of post-indus- trial economic scarcity. He suggests that hunter/gatherer economies were premised rather on an assumption of abundance and that they enjoyed a kind of material plenty. Their nomadic lifestyle attempted to ensure this. While leaner times were acknowledged, there was a fundamental belief that good seasons would return. While recent Australian research (reported in Altman 1991) in the post European contact situation has challenged Sahlins' notion of the 'original affluent society' (if affluence is measured in work-effort terms), there is evidence that despite differential resource bases, hunter-gatherer systems and techniques across the conti- nent were extremely flexible. Chase and Sutton (1991) suggest that many Australian environments were so rich in resources, particularly coastal and riverine, that movements by small groups of people were regular and largely predictable over a relatively small localised seasonal range, all resources being within a day's walk. Reynolds gives a graphic description of the differences in European and Aboriginal thinking and orientation. 'The big difference lay in the fact that they (Aborigines) did not see the need to sit around and wait for the crops to grow. Confident in their knowledge of the environment and their ability to ensure, by appropriate ritual, its continued flowering, they arranged their timetable to return to an area when a new crop had matured and ripened' (1983:142). It is important to note that increase rites were significant for both natural and social reproduction. However, this view changed following European invasion:chronic insecurity apparently increased the desire to preserve and stockpile food. 'As old certainties vanished, clans sought new ways to maintain their food supply' (Reynolds 1983:51). Neidjie of the Gagadju people asserts this notion of assumed plenty: 'All these places for us ... all belong Gagadju. We use them all the time. Old people used to move around, camp different place. Wet season, dry season ... always camp different place ... Everybody camp, like holiday. Plenty food this place.' (1985:40–1).

It should be noted that unusual night sky events have been recorded from the perspective of European astronomy.

Eclipses

An eclipse of the sun was a feared event and among the Aranda, it was greeted with great dread and trepidation. They thought that an eclipse was caused by periodic visits of the *Arungquilta*, a term used to refer to 'an evil or malignant influence'. Narratives about *Arungquilta* suggest that it caused an eclipse by coming from its home in the west and trying to make an abode in the sun, threatening to permanently obliterate its light. This evil spirit could also take on the form of an animal. The *Arungquilta* could only be dragged out of the sun by the skill of traditional healers and it is thought that to date, they have done so very successfully. It is interesting to note that among the Aranda, the Magellanic Clouds are also regarded as being endowed with *Arungquilta* and were reputed to sometimes come down to earth and choke people whilst they were sleeping. *Arungquilta* also inhabited mushrooms and toadstools, and consequently they were not eaten. Arungquilta could also take the form of falling stars and could be seen streaking across the sky as lightning.[37] According to other narratives, the evil influence that caused an eclipse could take the form of a large black bird *tia*, which stood in front of the sun.[38]

Among the Ngadjuri people of the Eyre Peninsula in South Australia, an eclipse was seen to be the result of the killing of an old cannibal woman and her dogs by two lizard men. One of the lizard men subsequently got the sun back by throwing a boomerang to the east.[39]

In northwestern Arnhem Land, an eclipse of the sun was seen as the Sun Woman being covered by the Moon Man in the act of copulation.[40] However, there is a myth which indicates that when the moon is

37 Spencer and Gillen 1966:415–6.
38 Strehlow 1907:19.
39 Tindale 1974:135.
40 Warner 1937:538.

in eclipse, it is seen as being his persistent lover, the sun, threatening to pursue and overtake him. The moon always succeeds in escaping.[41]

An eclipse of the moon among the Aranda was seen to be caused by the Moon Man hiding his face behind the possum fur which he was thought to be constantly spinning.[42] Among the Clarence River groups in New South Wales, an eclipse of the moon was thought to reveal the Moon Man's blood as the moon frequently appears red/orange during an eclipse.[43]

Halos

A halo around the moon held significance for the people of Mowanjum community in the Kimberleys.[44] It indicated the time when a boy was to be initiated. Among the Aranda, the appearance of a halo around the moon indicated that the Moon Man was spinning possum fur, rolling it with a flat hand on his upper leg.[45] Around the Clarence River area, the Moon Man (*Giwa*) was thought to have been killed while crossing the Culgoa River in the company of two women. However, he came back to life and invited many people from a neighbouring group to join him under a large sheet of leopard-wood bark (*Flindersai maculosa*), which he had propped up with forked branches. *Giwa* caused the bark to fall and everyone beneath it was killed. He rose to the sky to escape the inevitable vengeance which would be his lot. When a golden halo appeared around him, it was seen as his sheet of bark, (his reflection has been seen in leopard-wood bark ever since)[46] (also see Drawing 7 from Mabuiag in the Torres Strait.)

---

41 Reed (1965:130) does not indicate the location of this myth.

42 Strehlow 1907:21.

43 Mathews 1994:60.

44 Utemorrah et al 1980:46.

45 Strehlow 1907:21.

46 Mathews 1994:61.

Aurora Australis

The Aurora Australis can be seen from the southern parts of the continent in the direction south towards Antarctica and the South Magnetic Pole. It was seen by some Gippsland groups in Victoria[47] as the fire of an ancestral hero proclaiming catastrophes and wars. Its southern sky flames were also noted by the Dieri of the Lake Eyre region, indicated in a dictionary of their language[48] wherein the word for 'Aurora Australis' was literally translated to mean 'a charcoal fire of indignation, an angry blaze'. Among western Victorian groups, the word for the Aurora Australis was *puae buae*, meaning 'ashes'.[49]

Comets

Comets[50] appear to have evil portent in many societies, including those in Europe up until quite recently. Among the Pitjantjatjara people, comets were known as *wurluru*, and were seen as representing a large ancestral man who lived alone and occasionally hurled his spear across the darkened heavens. He was thought to be a ferociously powerful person, but not without redeeming qualities. He was both feared and respected and local tradition had it that he should not be looked at for long periods of time or he would cause the eyes to spin around.[51] An appearance of a comet in the early nineteenth century was regarded as a warning of impending catastrophe by South Australian groups,[52] as discussed earlier. Among western Victorian groups, comets were thought

---

47 Worms 1986:112.

48 Prepared by S Gason in Worms 1986:112.

49 Dawson 1981:101.

50 Comet' is a word derived from the Greek, *aster kometes*, meaning 'hairy stars'.

51 Raymo (1986:6), when visiting Uluru to see the 1986 return of Halley's Comet found this to be true!

52 Reynolds 1983:89.

to be the representations of a great spirit.[53] A comet seen at Mapoon in Queensland in May 1901 was believed to have been caused by a fire lit by two old women.[54] And among the Aranda and Luritja groups of Central Australia, comets were seen as spears thrown by an ancestral hero in his attempt, through magical practices, to make his wife obedient to him.[55]

Meteorites or Shooting Stars

Shooting stars, frequently represented in myth, were variously perceived across the continent. Among the Walbiri, for example, it was thought that sacred places on earth had fallen out of the Milky Way as shooting stars.[56] They were also seen as the way by which traditional healers could return from their sky-world visits,[57] as being important in the process of making healers[58] and as being a signal that exorcism in a healing ritual had been completed and was successful.[59] There is evidence that they also heralded to a prospective father, the approach of his newborn child. It was a sign that the spirit-child was 'moving on the sky-path to be born to the man's wife'.[60]

Shooting stars were also regarded as a sign that someone had died,[61] as the discarding of a shell when a fish (the star) died,[62] or as a manifestation of a spirit ancestor, *Nimparipari* of the Bathurst and Melville

53 Dawson 1981:101.

54 Roth 1984(5):8.

55 Strehlow 1907:30.

56 Warlukurlangu Artists 1987:127.

57 Gunson 1974:52.

58 Elkin 1945:86.

59 In the Wellessley Islands, Cawte 1974:110.

60 Harney and Elkin 1949:142.

61 Rose 1992:70; Peck 1933:169; Montagu 1974:155; Piddington 1932:394.

62 Piddington 1932:394.

Islands.[63] The Tiwi of these islands saw a shooting star as the single eye of the one-eyed spirit men, who made it their business to steal bodies and suck out their blood. The evil eyes that streaked across the sky were looking for their next prey.[64] On the Pilbara, a shooting star was seen as a long-legged goanna.[65] Among the Plangermairrener people of Tasmania, shooting stars were seen as the women *Puggareetya* thrown across the sky by Snake on whom she used to play tricks.[66] And a meteor among western Victorian groups was considered to be a 'deformity'.[67]

A myth whose only location is somewhere 'in (NSW) basalt country'[68] explains that a shooting star indicated that someone had taken a waratah from ground that did not belong to him or her. Apparently, the Aborigines used to bring waratah stems to the blacksmiths in the early days of the colony because 'they thought that the sparks from the anvil were the same fire as that that came from the sky'.[69] In another myth that explains the origin of the redness of flowers such as the waratah, there was a notion that stars 'loosened from their holds came flashing to earth', and that fragments of the red, glowing molten masses were received into certain plants giving them their redness.[70]

In the Bloomfield River area of Queensland, falling stars were likened to moving (bird-like) firesticks, and called *gi-we*. When a person fell sick and was far from his home country, his or her fellow travellers would throw a lighted firestick up into the night sky in the direction

---

63 Berndt and Berndt 1974:81.

64 Haynes 1992:139.

65 von Brandenstein and Thomas 1975:3, 57.

66 Everett in Noonuccal 1990:115–19.

67 Dawson 1981:101.

68 Peck 1925:79–86; 1933:160–6.

69 Peck 1933:168.

70 Peck (1933:202–3) seems to have confused the Magellanic Clouds with the dark patches in the Milky Way (1933:203), although in the seventeenth century, the dark patches were called *Macula Magellani*, Black Magellanic Cloud.

of the sick person. The relatives would hear them cry and see the message and know that one of their kinsmen or women was ill.[71] If a falling star fell to earth around the Brisbane area at a time of inter-group conflict, it was regarded as a sign that someone sick was doomed, as it was seen as the enemy's firestick falling down. The Tully River people in Queensland also saw falling stars as firesticks of the spirits of deceased enemies who did such things as starting bush fires. A falling star also meant the advent of any enemy and, if a person saw one, he or she was obliged to shout and make as much noise as possible. The following morning, a group would venture out in the direction of the meteorite to look for tracks of their 'would-be destroyer'.[72] Around Proserpine, a falling star indicated that an enemy had been killed, whereas around Pennefather River, people saw it as a female spirit of a deceased person pouring water over yams to help them grow. Around Bloomfield in Queensland, falling stars were thought to be quartz crystals.[73]

Among the Ngalia people of Central Australia, meteorites were seen as glowing stones thrown down to earth by the *Walanari*, two ancestral men whose camps were in the Magellanic Clouds. They threw down meteors to express their pleasure at totemic rituals being performed in their honour, or contrarily, displeasure when they thought they were being discussed inappropriately.[74] The *Walanari* punished evil-doers and rewarded those who kept the law. Among the Aranda and Luritja groups of Central Australia, meteorites were considered to be large venomous snakes (*kulaia*) with big, fiery eyes. They flew through the air and dropped into waterholes, thus making the waterholes places to be avoided.[75]

A meteor shower appeared to be significant in a myth explaining the arrival of the first kangaroo among south-eastern New South Wales

---

71 Roth 1983(5):8.

72 Roth 1983(5):8.

73 Roth 1983(5):8.

74 Mountford 1976b:457.

75 Strehlow 1907:30.

Aboriginal people living around Mount Kosciusko, Goulburn, the Currockbilly Ranges, Mittagong, Burragorang, Kiama and the Nepean River.

> A night in the daytime descended in a second, blotting out everything. But in the heavens a wondrous light appeared. Long streams of liquid fire started from the south, and shot sheer across the heavens from pole to pole. They waved from west to east. Red and yellow, purple and brown, pink and grey, golden and black, white and pale green. All these stretched from pole to pole, waved and crossed, and passed away towards the east.[76]

Earthshine[77]

The phenomenon of earthshine, or ashen light, was seen among the Tiwi of Bathurst and Melville Islands, as the spirit of Japara the Moon Man who regularly dies as a result of his excessive behaviour of eating too many mangrove crabs.[78]

Crepuscular Rays and Arches

Crepuscular rays and arches, as well as being, among some groups, paths to the Land of the Dead, were also seen as heralding distinctive twilights. Among western Victorian groups, for example, a crepuscular arch in the west in the morning was known as 'peep-of-the-day'; an upper was known as a 'black cockatoo twilight' and was thought to come from the constellation of Orion. The crepuscular rays in the west were known as 'rushes of the sun'.[79]

---

76 Smith 1992:21–3.

77 Earthshine is sunlight reflected from earth. Close to new moon, earthshine reflected by the moon back to the earth enables the whole lunar disk to become visible, the old moon in the new moon's arms.

78 Roberts and Mountford 1974:100.

79 Dawson 1981:101.

Terrestrial Luminescence/Phosphorescence

In the Forrest River area, west of Wyndham in north-west Australia, phosphorescence in the water was seen as evidence of the presence of the Rainbow Serpent.[80]

Glow-worms

Among western Victorian groups, it was a common notion that glow-worms took their light from Butt *kuee tuukuung*, Antares (*Alpha Scorpii*), whose name meant 'big stomach'.[81]

A curious, observant and philosophical people, the Australian Aborigines had a deep interest in their natural surroundings. The night sky was an extension of the terrestrial landscape and thus was of equal interest to them. It also acted both as a projection of social and intellectual life as well as a source of inspiration to them. Their astronomical knowledge, although not a separate or discrete epistemology, was nevertheless, detailed and extensive. It was significant to all aspects of their cultural life.

---

80 Elkin 1930:350.
81 Dawson 1981:99.

Bark Paintings 1

(from Mountford, Melbourne University Press, 1956)

The Milky Way, Millingimbi

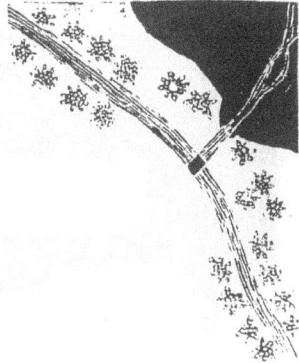

The Milky Way and Coal Sack, Oenpelli

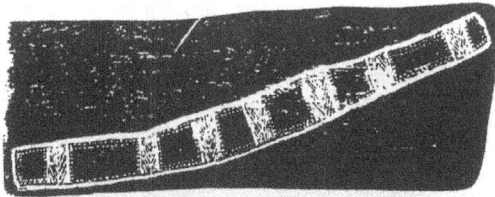

The Milky Way, Groote Eylandt

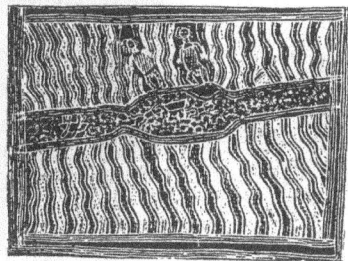

The Milky Way, Yirrkala

Bark Paintings 2

(from Mountford, Melbourne, University Press, 1956)

Orion and the Pleiades, Yirrkala

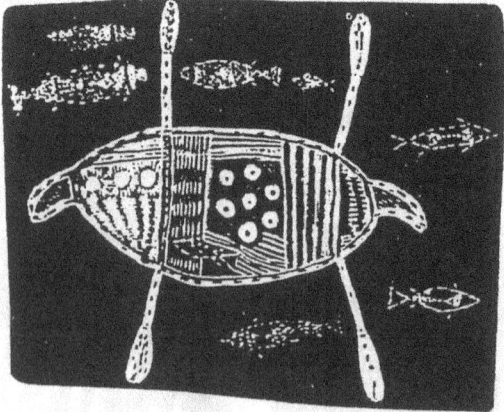

Orion and the Pleiades, Millingimbi

Bark Paintings 3

(from Mountford, Melbourne University Press, 1956)

Orion and the Pleiades, Groote Eylandt

Bark Paintings 4

(from Mountford, Melbourne University Press, 1956)

The Magellan Clouds, Yirrkala

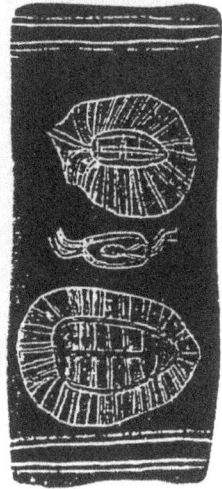

(Above) The Magellan Clouds, Groote Eylandt

(Left) The Southern Cross and Pointers, Yirrkala

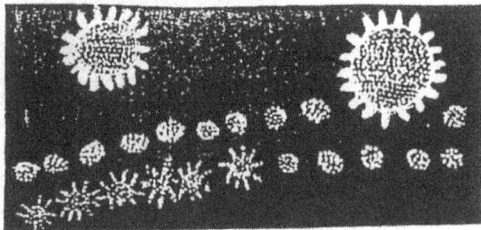

The Morning Stars, Oenpelli

Bark Paintings 5

(from Mountford, Melbourne University Press, 1956)

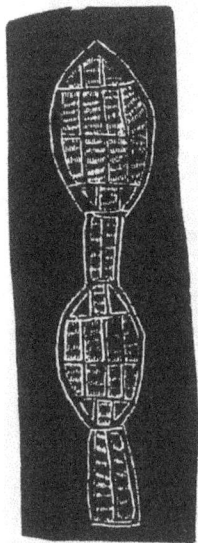

The Sun Woman, Groote Eylandt

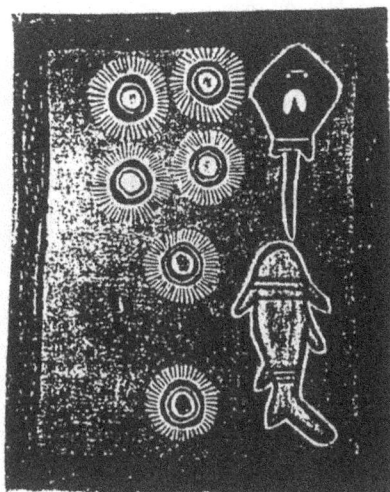

Venus, Jupiter and their Children, Groote Eyland

The Sun Woman, Yirrkala

Bark Paintings 6

(from Mountford, Melbourne University Press, 1956)

The Moon Man, Yirrkala

Bark Paintings 7

(from Mountford, Melbourne University Press, 1956)

The Moon Man, Millingimbi

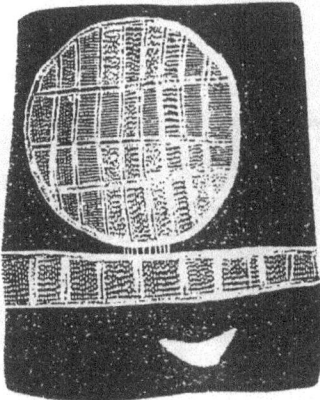

The Moon Man, Groote Eylandt

Bark Paintings 8

(from Mountford, Melbourne University Press, 1956)

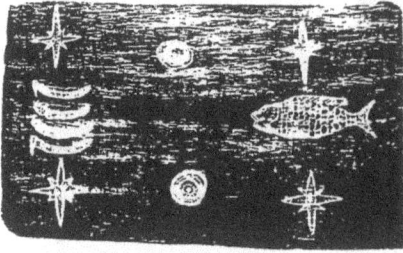

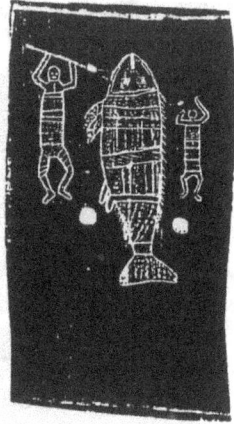

The Southern Cross, Groote Eylandt

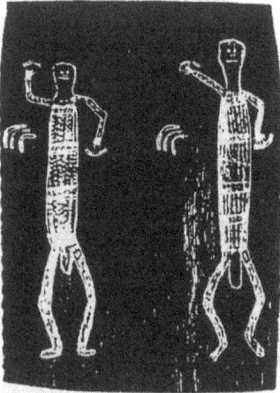

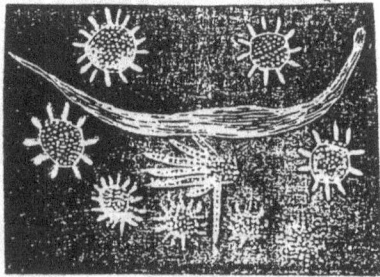

The Southern Cross, Oenpelli

The Pointers, Groote Eylandt

Bark Paintings 9

(from Mountford, Melbourne University Press, 1956)

The Crab, Groote Eylandt

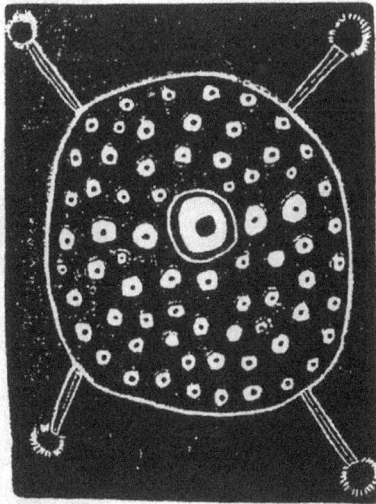

Walagugu and the Tjirupun, Oenpelli

Bark Paintings 10

(from Mountford, Melbourne University Press, 1956)

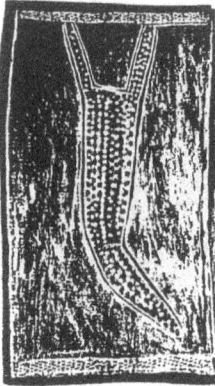

The Scorpion, Yirrkala

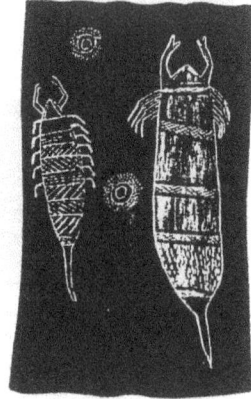

The Scorpions, Groote Eylandt

The Opossum Man, Kapali, Oenpelli

The Crocodile, the Opossum
and the Ibis Men, Yirrkala

8

The Fall of the Sky-Dome

Ideas about the Aboriginal cosmos clearly changed and evolved over time. However, European invasion and settlement provided an impetus to change, in catastophic proportions. The cosmologist Harrison has suggested that all universes conceived by humans are 'impermanent conceptual schemes' rising, flourishing and then declining over time to be finally superseded.[1] Their decline and fall were usually due to one of four reasons.[2] The first cause was assault by an alien culture; the second was because startling new discoveries produced new notions; the third was because old problems re-emerged, refusing to stay submerged; and the fourth was because there was a relentless shift in public opinion. Yet, throughout history, in all cultures, there is and has always been a conviction by participants that a particular cultural conception of the universe is *the* Universe, their particular mask the true face. According to Harrison:

> Each universe or mask presents a conceptual scheme that organises human thought and shapes human understanding. Generally, within each universe, the end to the search for all knowledge at last looms in sight. Each universe, in its day flourished as an awe-inspiring, self consistent scheme of thought, yet each is doomed to be superseded by another and perhaps grander scheme.[3]

Harrison identifies the Australian Aboriginal universe, before white contact, as being a 'magico-mythic universe'.[4] The sudden arrival of

---

1 Harrison 1985:13.

2 Harrison 1985:2.

3 Harrison 1985:vii.

4 In the 'magicomythic universe', the world possessed exalted spirits which reflected not only the characteristics of human beings, but also

Europeans in the landscape had to be made sense of by the Aboriginal occupants.

The arrival at first sparked more curiosity than fear. It provoked 'intense and often prolonged debate as to the true nature of the white men, their origin and objectives'.[5] There was a pervasive idea across the length and breadth of the continent that Europeans were returning spirits of the dead. Because the cosmos of the Aborigines was geographically limited, all people known to any individual were regarded as kin or potential kin. So the white strangers were initially perceived as kin and in many cases, not just reincarnated souls, but actual identifiable countrymen (and occasionally women). The whiteness of skin colour appeared, at least initially, to support the view of the return of the dead because white was a colour widely associated with death and used extensively in mourning rituals.[6]

In an account by the explorer, George Grey in 1841, he reports how he was perceived as the reincarnated son of an old Aboriginal woman:

> A sort of procession came up, headed by two women, down whose cheeks tears were streaming. The eldest of these came up to me, and looking for a moment at me ... 'Yes, yes, in truth it is him;' and then throwing her arms around me, cried bitterly, her head resting on my breast; and although I was totally ignorant of what their meaning was, from mere motives of compassion, I offered no resistance to her caresses ... At last the old lady, emboldened by my submission, deliberately kissed me on each cheek ... she then cried a little more, and at length relieving me, assured me that I was the ghost of her son, who had some time before been killed by a spear wound in his breast ... My new mother expressed almost as much

---

those of the institutions of their societies. Through the intercession of these exalted spirits, humans could gain some semblance of control over their world. (Harrison 1985:28).

5 Reynolds 1983:30.

6 Bates 1992:169; Lawrie 1970:323; Roth 1984 (5):16; Reynolds 1983:31–2; Strehlow 1907:16.

delight at my return to my family, as my real mother would
have done, had I been unexpectedly restored to her.[7]

Because of this perception, which fitted the social and physical order
of their worldview, the Aborigines were initially curious and friendly to
the Europeans,[8] and castaway mariners and escapee convicts, such as
Morrell, Buckley and Thompson, were accepted and taken in, even if
treated as simpletons as a result of their cultural ignorance and naivety.
The Aborigines also expected the whites to return from whence they
came: they certainly did not expect a permanent and ongoing, extended
visit, let alone occupation.

To explain the presence of these returned spirits, Massola[9] reports
a story which grew out of these perceptions held by Aboriginal people
and the particular historical circumstances. This version of the story
originated among Aboriginal groups in Victoria:

> The solid vault of the sky was believed to rest on props
> placed at the extreme edges of the earth. The eastern prop
> was supposed to be in (the) charge of an old man who lived
> on the High Plains. Berak, the last of the Yarra tribe, stated
> that when he was a boy news came to his people by way of
> the Ovens River and Goulburn River blacks, that the east-
> ern prop was rotting, and that if presents were not sent to
> the old man in charge, he would not repair it, the sky would
> fall, and everybody would be killed. He stated that this news
> filled the land with consternation, and that many possum
> rugs and stone axes were sent eastwards. This incident is also
> mentioned by Buckley, the escaped convict. He affirmed that
> the people he was with on the Barwon River, told him they
> had passed the news on to other tribes along the coast, and
> that many presents were sent. A similar message was passed
> from tribe to tribe along the Murray River. The Wotjobaluk
> believed that the sky rested on props which not only held it

7 In Reynolds 1983:34.

8 Willey 1979:50–1.

9 Massola 1968:105.

up, but also allowed the sun to pass underneath the lid, to
light and warm the earth.[10]

The danger in all these stories was seen as coming from the east,
the direction from which the invaders had initially come, and were
continuing to come. There was a clear inference in these stories that
the eastern support had rotted and given way and the sky had fallen
down.[11] As a result, the spirits or reincarnations of all the Aborigines
who had ever lived had broken through from the spirit world and were
swarming over the land. Death and catastrophe were indeed imminent.
The anthropologist, Kenneth Maddock, has remarked that: 'Given the
unity of society and their cosmology, it is not to be wondered at that the
impending ruin of their social order should be prefigured in the fear
that the cosmos was about to collapse upon them.'[12]

Another story in the same vein has surfaced. Mudrooroo Nyoongah
tells the story of *Djangan*, the greatest hero of the Nyoongah people of
south-western Western Australia. One day, *Djangan* was sitting near a
causeway (now Fremantle), fishing. Europeans (*watjelas*) were around
and were regarded with great fear as they were seen as ghosts (*djangara*)
who were particularly troublesome because they were head-hunters.
Europeans trapped *Djangan*, shot him and then hacked off his head with
a tomahawk. 'One, two, three blows and it was off at his neck. Then, they
smoked it, just like you smoke a ham. They sent it off to England to add
to the collection they had there. It was part of their magic, part of their
empire, collecting skulls'.[13] For many of the Aboriginal people, the sky
of their world really did fall down.

Much of the traditional lands of the Aboriginal people was gradually taken over for white settlement and, consequently, accessible
places known to be good for hunting, fishing and gathering were greatly

---

10 Massola 1979:55

11 Roberts and Mountford 1974:55.

12 Maddock 1974:55.

13 In Noonuccal 1990:177–8.

diminished.[14] The Aboriginal people of the northern Kimberleys attributed the resulting severe food shortages to the immense powers of their creator spirit, *Galalang*, an all-father creator spirit, who lived in the dark spot between the European constellations Centaurus and Scorpius.[15] Before he departed for the sky-world, *Galalang* gave the Aboriginal people 'the best country, the most beautiful language, a long life and monogamous marriage'. Apparently offended by the way people were behaving, *Galalang* dried up a lake of good water where fish and turtles had been in abundance. With a tree trunk behind him,[16] he dug a canal and let the daily food of the Aboriginal people escape to the sea. Presumably, he then returned to his dark patch in the Milky Way.

Sally Morgan, a contemporary Aboriginal writer and painter,[17] has cast a rather whimsical eye over the coming of whites. In a story of her own making,[18] she suggests that the first white man came about as a result of an Aboriginal boy turning white with fear after he disobeyed tradition and his mother's warnings in particular. A giant fish called Munka regularly terrorised a lake between the hours of midnight to dawn, and the boy ignored his mother's injunction:

When darkness falls and the sky is black,

And the stars all blink with fright,

Munka comes up with his open mouth

In the middle of the night.

'Food!' he screams. 'I want food! Any child will do!

I'll snap him up and crunch his bones and grind him into stew!'

---

14 The resulting severe food shortages are well documented by Reynolds (1983).

15 Worms 1986:129.

16 Perhaps, suggests Worms, an allusion to the iron plough introduced by the Europeans.

17 Born in 1951 in Perth.

18 Morgan 1992:85–89.

The boy was swallowed whole by *Munka*, who fortunately gagged and vomited him up. To his dismay, the boy discovered he had turned white with terror.[19]

Gradually, the Aboriginal view of their cosmos was forced to take greater account of modern European and Christian ideologies. And too, traditional narratives underwent modifications and change with these influences, dogmas and images. Daphne Nimanydja from Arnhem Land, for example, retells an old story about the moon, *Ngalindi*, with a new twist. *Ngalindi* had two sons, who went on a successful fishing expedition, but on their return they refused to share the catch with their father. The moon put the two boys into a canoe, paddled out to the deep and threw them in. The mothers of the boys returned from gathering yams and, believing their sons to have been at least harmed in some way, or even killed by their husband, they 'belted him up'! The moon, trying to escape their wrath, climbed higher and higher up a tall tree.

> It's (the) same thing that when Jesus died on the cross, he rose again, the same way that *Ngalindi*, when he dies, he comes back, you know, he came back in the (full) new moon—same thing happened for *Ngalindi*, like Jesus died on the cross and he rose again. And that's the story we use, for the community at Millingimbi.[20]

Attempts by the surviving Aboriginal people to explain the European invasion and its continuing, all pervasive influence have been ongoing. Why Hermannsburg (Ntaria) was chosen to be the particular site of the first German Lutheran missionary activity, for instance, is the subject of much local speculation. Aranda narratives of the Lutheran encounter include the notion that a shooting star designated the place. This star motif links the Aranda people to the (Christian) star of Bethlehem, and

---

19 Perhaps white men are a personification of Aboriginal fear. A version of this story is reported by Roth (1984 (5):16 from the Pennefather River area in Queensland. The monstrous creature in this case was a huge brown serpent and the boy escaped the serpent's belly by being excreted. The loss of his skin resulted in him becoming white.

20 In Davis and Hodge 1985:99–100.

so explains and fixes their particular 'Church of Bethlehem'.[21] There is, even today, a representation of the star in rock markings on a hill near Palm Valley. [22]

As we move into the twenty first century, the cosmologist Harrison makes a timely observation[23]: 'Adrift like shipwrecked mariners, in a vast and meaningless mechanistic universe, we are found clinging for life to the cosmos wreckage of ancient universes.'

---

21 Austin-Broos 1994:140.

22 According to Austin-Broos, stories about the falling star may also involve associations with a Deamtime story about a star which fell to earth in Palm Valley.

23 Harrison 1985:117.

Epilogue

Stars, it seems, still play a very significant role in the lives of Aboriginal and Torres Strait Islander people. Their appearance quite recently in a well-lit and highly scrubbed court room of the nation's capital illustrates well the importance Aboriginal people still attach to their customary beliefs and practices.

The much celebrated *Mabo* Case concluded on 3 June 1992 with a resounding victory for the Meriam people of the Torres Strait Island of Mer (Murray Island), when six of the seven High Court judges ruled that the Meriam people 'are entitled as against the whole world to possession, occupation, use, and enjoyment of the island of Mer'.[1] The Meriam people's claim to native title was recognised and became a precedent for mainland Aboriginal people in their ongoing struggle for recognition of land rights, as well as effectively ending the fiction of *terra nullius*.

During the court case itself, extensive evidence was taken about traditional law concerning the continuity of principles of land ownership, as set down by Malo (an ecologically oriented spirit ancestor, *Malo ra Gelar* in the Meriam language). Malo's Law as explained by the plaintiffs to the court, is a *lived* law, interwoven into the fabric of everyday life, and handed down orally from one generation to the next.[2] Malo's Law includes laws against trespass, laws about keeping to one's secret ways, laws prescribing that the land be productive under cultivation and laws demanding that unneeded fruit be left to drop to the ground. Interestingly, most of the plaintiffs delivered the allegorical invocation

1 Except for the land previously leased to the Anglican Church's Australian board of Missions. *Mabo and Others v the State of Queensland and the Commonwealth of Australia* in the High Court of Australia, 3 June 1962, Judgement per Brennan J. 66 Australian Law Journal Reports.

2 Sharp 1994:7,15–16.

'Stars follow their own path', when asked about land tenure, succession and trespass. The invocation directly addresses all three.[3]

This invocation is inspired, as an ongoing source of instruction, by the vast night time constellation of the *Tagai*, the ancient sea hero, as previously discussed. Since ancient times, he has represented the charter for the Meriam people, to follow their own cultural traditions inherited from their forebears, and which in due course, they must pass on to the next generation. And as a corollary, they must not trespass or encroach on what does not rightly belong to them: 'I cannot walk the path that is *Usiam*'s (the Pleiades) nor can I walk the path that is *Seg*'s (Orion) ... for I must follow *teter mek*, the footprints made by my ancestors'.[4] From eons past, to this day, the *Tagai* represents this charter.

The continuing significance of the stars for the Meriam is profound, as the stars for them have their own ongoing course in the heavens, each star having its own journey to make. Likewise, everything has a place in the cosmos; its own time, its own place and its own destiny to fulfil.

Having lived with the Meriam, Nonie Sharp has made this comment: 'The pattern of (Meriam) social life ... is written in their layout of the stars. Its movement is inscribed in their trek across the sky. The pattern of the stars becomes the language of a cultural statement'.[5]

The rights and duties of the Meriam to their land are regarded by them as being sacred, backed up and given authority by other dimensions integrally linked to the land: totems, winds and, of course, the stars.[6]

When Edward Koiki Mabo left his home on Mer Island under the exhortation from one of the custodians of traditional culture—'whatever you do, Koiki, wherever you go, always remember (to) bring back the idea (you learn) to Murray Island'[7]—little did he know that, like a

---

3 Sharp 1994:7.

4 Lawrie 1937:373; Sharp 1993:71.

5 Sharp 1994:6.

6 Sharp 1994:19.

7 Sharp 1994:8.

star following its own path, he would bring back some thirty years later, even after his own personal demise, the great gift of native title. Koiki Mabo (as he is known by his people) became the first plaintiff in the landmark case which was to bear, posthumously, his name.

Appendices

Appendix 1: Aboriginal Constellations

Night sky phenomena (European)	Aboriginal mythological representation	Association	Aboriginal group or place	Source
Deneb (*Alpha Cygnus*), Capella (*Alpha Auriga*) and several pairs of faint stars between Auriga and Taurus	Native cat (*Pardjidja*) ,Deneb, and opossum (*Langgur*),Capella, and tracks of the opossum (faint stars).	Origin of markings on these animals	Karadjeri, north-western WA	Piddington 1932:395

Night sky phenomena (European)	Aboriginal mythological representation	Association	Aboriginal group or place	Source
Magellanic Clouds, Canopus (*Alpha Carinae*), Sirius (*Alpha Canis Majoris*) and two (undesignated) stars	The Magellanic Clouds are the spirits of two ancestral heroes. *Bagadjimbiri*, Canopus and Sirius represent two women, *Yerinyeri* and *Wolabun*, who collect food together on earth but *Yerinyeri* continually teases *Wolabun* about snakes. *Wolabun*, in revenge, places a dead water snake in a pond which scares *Yeriyeri*. Both women flee to the sea before going to the sky. *Bulian*, the great water serpent is also in the sky and his eyes are represented by stars.	*Bulian* is associated with seasonal change	Karadjeri, WA	Piddington 1930:352–54
Sigma, Delta, Rho, Zeta and Eta Hydrae	These stars form *Unwala*, an ancestral crab		Groote Eylandt, NT	Mountford 1956:479
Venus, Jupiter, Lambda and Upsilon Scorpii	Venus, a man (*Barnimbida*), and Jupiter, a woman (*Duwardwara*), have two children, *Lambda* and *Upsilon Scorpii*.	Strong, south-easterly winds which blow during April	Groote Eylandt, NT	Mountford 1956:481

Night sky phenomena (European)	Aboriginal mythological representation	Association	Aboriginal group or place	Source
Small (undesignated) stars in Lynx, and two large stars in Lynx (probably *Alpha* and *Beta Lyncis*)	Small stars in Lynx are scorpions, old childless star-people who hunt and fish over the sky. They cook over their own fires, *Alpha* and *Beta Lyncis*.		Groote Eylandt, NT	Mountford 1956:481
Magellanic Clouds and Achernar (*Alpha Eridani*)	The Magellanic Clouds are the camps of an old man and a woman (the *Jukara*) who cannot gather their own food. Achernar is their fire.	Tides	Groote Eylandt, NT	Mountford 1956:484–85
The Southern Cross, *Alpha* and *Beta Centauri* and the Coal Sack	Coal Sack is a fish, *Alakitja*, speared by two brothers, *Alpha* and *Beta Crucis*. Their fires are *Gamma* and *Delta Crucis*. Their friends are *Alpha* and *Beta Centauri*.	Rock cod	Groote Eylandt, NT	Mountford 1956:485–87
(Unidentified) October morning stars, the Milky Way and the Coal Sack	A celestial family (*Garakma*) feed on waterlily bulbs from the Milky Way and from a fruit tree in the Coal Sack.		Oenpelli, NT	Mountford 1956:487

163

Night sky phenomena (European)	Aboriginal mythological representation	Association	Aboriginal group or place	Source
Southern Cross and the Coal Sack	*Nangurgal*, a group of starmen (large stars in the Cross) and their sons (smaller stars in the Cross) catch a snake and eat it. The snake is the Coal Sack. The stars of the cross are the bright eyes of the men.		Oenpelli, NT	Mountford 1956:487
Orion, the Hyades, the Pleiades, some stars of Gemini and some stars of Eridanus	Constellation of the Canoe Stars, visible December to March.		Millingimbi, NT	Mountford 1956:495–6
Southern Cross and Pointers *Alpha* and *Beta Centauri*	Southern Cross is a stingray eternally pursued by the Pointers which represent a shark.		Galbu (Caldeon Bay), NT	Mountford 1956:496
Stars of Lupus	Scorpion		Yirrkala, NT	Mountford 1956:500

Night sky phenomena (European)	Aboriginal mythological representation	Association	Aboriginal group or place	Source
Magellanic Clouds	Camps of two sisters. The elder sister and her dog live in the Large Magellanic Cloud and the younger sister and her dog life in the Small Magellanic Cloud. The elder sister is believed to leave as only the Small Magellanic Cloud is visible during the dry season, April to September, whereas both are visible during the wet season.		Yirrkala, NT	Mountford 1956:500
Arcturus (*Alpha Bootis*) Saak (*Eta Bootis*) and the Moon	Arcturus is a man and Saak a woman.	Dugong, Pandanus *rakia* (spike-thrush) and tides	Millingimbi, NT	Mountford 1956:495–96
Dark Patch (in the Milky Way between Centaurus and Scorpius), *Alpha* and *Beta Centauri*	*Galalang*, an ancestral hero lives in the dark patch. *Alpha* and *Beta Centauri* are two feathers from his headdress, one white from a parrot, the other dark from an owl.	Creation hero	Western Kimberley, WA	Worms 1986:129 Durak 1969:77

Night sky phenomena (European)	Aboriginal mythological representation	Association	Aboriginal group or place	Source
Stars in Canis Major	Wunbula, a Bat, had his two wives, a Brown Snake (*Murrbumbool*) and a Black Snake (*Moondtha*) impaled on spears for trying to get rid of him by burying him alive. They all went to the sky and the constellation is known as *Munowra*.		Dharumba, Shoalhaven River area, NSW	Ridley 1875:144–45
Antares (*Alpha Scorpii*) and the Milky Way	Flying foxes (Milky Way) were angry with *Purupriki*, a tribal man (Antares), who attacked them. The flying foxes carried *Purupriki* away.			Roberts and Mountford 1974:32
Southern Cross and Beta Centauri	*Mululu (Beta Centauri)*, a tribal leader, arranged for his four daughters (the stars of the Cross) to climb up to him on the beard of a healer, *Conduk*.		Kanda	Roberts and Mountford 1974:76

Night sky phenomena (European)	Aboriginal mythological representation	Association	Aboriginal group or place	Source
Southern Cross, *Alpha* and *Beta Centauri*	The Southern Cross is the camp of two mothers and their fires are the Pointers. They came to earth in search of food. The fire sticks they carried got out of control. The fire which ensued was captured by people on earth.	Origin and ownership of fire	North-western coast WA, NSW north coast	Roberts and Mountford 1974:94 Ellis 1991:75–77
The Pointers, *Alpha* and *Beta Centauri*	Escape of two creation heroes, the Pointers, from bushfire.	Creation of Flinders Ranges	Flinders Ranges, SA	Roberts and Mountford 1974:114 Tunbridge 1988:74
Morning Star (Venus)	Two hawk-men (eagles) who are creation heroes live in the Morning Star.	Creation heroes	Lake Torrens, SA	Worms 1986:134

Night sky phenomena (European)	Aboriginal mythological representation	Association	Aboriginal group or place	Source
Morning Star (Venus) and unspecified stars	Two sons were disrespectful to their father and so were punished. The father became the Morning Star and never again associated with his sons who were turned into stars along with their clubs and kangaroos.	Power of elders	Flinders Ranges, SA	Roberts and Mountford 1974:118 Tunbridge 1988:122–3
Two dark patches in the Milky Way	Evil spirit, *Waiwera*, abducts a beautiful young dancer named Brolga, and sweeps her up in a willy-willy. She returns to earth changes into a Brolga. *Waiwera* lives in the dark patches.		Mandalbingu of Arnhem Land, NT	Rule and Goodman 1979:36–45

Night sky phenomena (European)	Aboriginal mythological representation	Association	Aboriginal group or place	Source
Long line of dark patches (in Milky Way between *Alpha Centauri* and *Alpha Cygnus*), the Pleiades, the Gemini twins, Castor and Pollux (*Alpha* and *Beta Geminorum*), and Procyon (*Alpha Canis Minoris*)	The dark patches represent a large totem board which was made by two ancestral men, the *Wati Kutjara*, while on a journey with the Pleiades women. Castor and Pollux, their firesticks, are carried by a man, *Tangi*, who is represented by Procyon.	Sexual antagonism	Ngadadjara, Warburton Ranges, WA	Tindale 1936:169, 185
Aldebaran (*Alpha Tauri*)	*Karambal*, a man (*Alpha Tauri*), absconded with another man's wife. He was pursued by the husband and took refuge in a tree. The pursuer set the tree on fire, the flames of which carried *Karambal* into the sky. He still retains the colour of the fire.	Kinship laws	Clarence River area, NSW	Mathews 1905:78

Night sky phenomena (European)	Aboriginal mythological representation	Association	Aboriginal group or place	Source
Lambda and *Upsilon Scorpii*, Altair (*Alpha Aquilae*), the Northern Crown (*Corona Borealis*), and Venus	*Lambda* and *Upsilon Scorpii* represent a crow. Altair is a great hunter, *Wukkarno*, who had several dogs and a boomerang (Northern Crown). Venus is a man (*Mirnkabuli*), who lives in a grass 'gurli' and subsists on mussels and crayfish.		Darling River, NSW	Mathews 1905:81
Antares (*Alpha Scorpii*) and Jupiter	Antares is an Eaglehawk. Jupiter is a great man, *Wurndawurnda-yarroa*, who lived on roasted yams.		Victorian groups	Massola 1971:41–45
Altair (*Alpha Aquilae*), (*Alpha Capricorni*) and Achernar (*Alpha Eridani*)	Altair is a great warrior, *Thattyukul*, who, while pursuing a codfish, created the Murray River. In the process, he injured his mother-in-law (*Alpha Capricorni*), who took revenge and disowned him. He was then rescued and revived by his uncle, represented by Achernar.	Creation of Murray River	Murray River area in NSW/Victoria	Mathews 1905:81–84

Night sky phenomena (European)	Aboriginal mythological representation	Association	Aboriginal group or place	Source
Antares (*Alpha Scorpii*) and the two stars either side (probably *Tau* and *Sigma Scorpii*)	Antares, an eaglehawk, *Gwarmbilla*, had two wives, a mallee-hen and a whip-snake. *Gulabirra*, a lizard-man wanted the wives and they him. The wives, when the eagle was out hunting, left the camp and dug a hole. They put bone spikes in it and filled it with their blood. They covered it to appear as a bandicoot's nest. The eagle was sent to the trap and fell in. His mother pulled him out, covered red with blood (he has been ever since). The mother took the two wives and put them either side of the eagle so they could never stray again. These stars always come up in the east before winter.	Winter	Wongaibon, NSW	Mathews nd.:4, 46, 55–6
Southern Cross, Magellanic Clouds, the Pleiades and Venus	Eaglehawk (Southern Cross) who has his camp in the Magellanic Clouds, chases the Pleiades women. Venus is a woman who came to earth and left a stone, as a reminder.	Sexual antagonism	Wolmeri, WA	Kaberry 1939:12

Night sky phenomena (European)	Aboriginal mythological representation	Association	Aboriginal group or place	Source
Southern Cross	An emu-man resides in the Southern Cross. His daughter was claimed by a giant on an island.		Yaoro, Broome area, WA	Durack 1969:238
Antares (Alpha Scorpii, Tau and Syma Scorpii and three stars underneath Sirius (Alpha Canis Majoris) and Delta, Epsilon and Zeta Orionis	The two stars either side of Antares are his wives, and the three stars underneath are 'nearly a grandfather' Sirius is a male eagle, whose sisters are the three stars in the belt of Orion. The eagle always follows them.		Western Victoria	Dawson 1981:99–100
Morning and Evening star, Venus	Munjarra, the morning and the evening star was a bright stone in a river before it went up to the sky. The sun insisted it could not stay around during the day. It goes to the sea until the tide washes it into the night sky.	Origin story	Djauan, NT	Robinson 1967:34
Two (undesignated) winter stars	Twin brothers wander across the sky, crying for their grandfather, their mother and their brother.		Gullibul, NSW	Robinson 1965:1965:51–58

Night sky phenomena (European)	Aboriginal mythological representation	Association	Aboriginal group or place	Source
The Pleiades, Orion and Venus	The *Mayi-mayi* were seven sisters with long hair and bodies of icicles. A large family of young men, the *Berai-Berai* (Orion) followed them wanting them as wives, but old *Warunna* stole two of the women, who finally escaped to their sisters. The *Berai-Berai* pined for the women and finally died. The *Mayi-mayi* break ice from their bodies and throw it down to earth as frost. Venus is a relative of the Mayi-mayi and when he saw *Warunna*'s defeat, he laughed with pleasure and is known as the 'Laughing Star.' Thunder in the winter-time is the women of the Pleiades bathing and playing.	Frost and winter rain	Kamilaroi, NSW NSW groups	Ridley 1875:141 Parker 1953:105–27

Night sky phenomena (European)	Aboriginal mythological representation	Association	Aboriginal group or place	Source
Magellanic Clouds, Alnitak, Alnelam and Mintaka (the stars in Orion's Belt), the Coalsack and Venus	Magellanic Clouds are fish, with Orion's belt representing a stick which broke off from a bull-roarer, which is the Coal Sack. (Women are not supposed to know of its existence.) Venus is a black bird.		Lunga, WA	Kaberry 1939:12
Stars in the tail of Scorpius, M7, and the star cluster below	An initiate and his lover flee from initiation rites into the sky (into the curl of the Scorpion's tail). The headdress of the initiate is M7. Two guardians of the boy follow. The star cluster (below M7) is a throwing stick belonging to the guardians.	Necessity of tribal law	Western Desert	Mountford 1948:165–66; 1976b:457–60
Magellanic Clouds, Achernar (*Alpha Eridani*), Canopus (*Alpha Carinae*)	Two sky heroes (Large Magellanic Cloud is the elder, when an Aboriginal person is dying, if the man or woman has been good or evil. If the person has been evil, the Large Magellanic Cloud spears the spirit and takes it to Achernar which is the campfire of the younger (Small Magellanic Cloud). After being cooked, it is eaten. If the person has been good, the elder intervenes to protect the spirit, and takes it to Canopus.	Good and evil	Western Desert, SA/NT	Mountford 1948:168

Night sky phenomena (European)	Aboriginal mythological representation	Association	Aboriginal group or place	Source
Coal Sack	Known as the 'Grandmother Spirit' (*Puckowe*).	Healing		Ramsay Smith 1939:184
Constellations of Delphinus, Lyra, Aquila, parts of Cygnus and parts of Hercules	This Aboriginal constellation is a family of crow-people. Vega (*Alpha Lyrae*) is the mother-crow who watches her son, Altair (*Alpha Aquilae*), showing off his new feather decorations which are placed on the top of each wing (a third-magnitude star to the east, and a fourth-magnitude star west, of Altair). Father-crow (Delphinus) watches. Aquila, Lyra, (arm of) Hercules and Albireo (*Gamma Cygni*) are footprints of members of the family and pieces of cooked meat.		Western Desert	Mountford 1948:168–69; 1976b:452–53

Night sky phenomena (European)	Aboriginal mythological representation	Association	Aboriginal group or place	Source
Coal Sack, the Southern Cross, the Pointers (*Alpha* and *Beta Centauri*), the 'false cross', *Pi* and *Sigma Argus* (now *Iota* and *Epsilon Carinae* and *Kappa* and *Sigma Puppis* - a 1932 revision by the International Astronomical Union Committee divided Argo Navis into Carina, Puppis and Vela)	The Coal Sack is the rest of the Wedgetailed eagle, *Waluwara* and the Southern Cross are his footprints. The Pointers are his throwing-stick. The 'false cross' in Carina and Vela is the footprint of the Kite-Hawk. (All the bright stars between the Southern Cross and the horizon at the time of the enquiry—9.00p.m. June 1940—were places where the eagle had once killed his prey.)		Western Desert	Mountford 1976b:450–51
Venus, Jupiter and Saturn	Two brothers and a dog. (Jupiter is the dog).		Western Desert	Mountford 1976b:450

Night sky phenomena (European)	Aboriginal mythological representation	Association	Aboriginal group or place	Source
Magellanic Clouds, Canopus (*Alpha Carinae*), *Alpha* and *Delta Pictoris*, Achernar (*Alpha Eridani*) *Beta* and *Delta Hydrus*	The large Magellanic Cloud is the camp of the elder *Kungara* brother. Canopus is the campfire and the two stars of Pictor represent his spear. The lesser Magellanic Cloud is the camp of the younger brother, Achernar is his campfire and the two stars in Hydra, his spear.	Good and evil after death	Western Desert and Ngalia of the Central Desert	Mountford 1976b:454–56
Double stars in Scorpius and (undesignated) iso-lated stars nearby	Young men climbed into the sky to bring back sacred objects from a cave in the double stars of Scorpius. Their footprints are the isolated stars nearby. The young men were unable to pull any of the sacred objects from the tightly packed pile. Three older men followed and took some of the objects from the outer ledge of the cave. For a long time, these were stored in one of the Mala caves on the northern side of Ayers Rock, but have been moved for safekeeping.	Sacred objects	Ayers Rock (Uluru), NT	Mountford 1976b:483

Night sky phenomena (European)	Aboriginal mythological representation	Association	Aboriginal group or place	Source
Dark patch	*Windaru*, a Bandicoot ancestral man stole sacred objects from the Milky Way. The objects used to rest in a dark patch in the Milky Way.	Sacred objects	Western Desert	Mountford 1976b:181
Veta (*Alpha Lyrae*), Sheliak (*Beta Lyrae*), Sulaphat (*Gamma Lyrae*), Altair (*Alpha Aquilae*) and Delphinus	Wega is *Wommainya*, holding out his long beard to rescue from drowning his two sons (Sheilak and Sulaphat). In his grief, he has speared to death his wife (Altair) and his wife's lazy brother (Delphinus). The lazy brother is condemned to sit beside his sister forever and not with the other men.	Care of children Marriage rules and kinship regulations	Ooldea region Bibbulmun people, south-western WA	Ker Wilson 1977:28–31 Bates 1992:170
Southern Cross and the Pointers (*Alpha* and *Beta Centauri*)	When a kangaroo was eaten without permission, an evil spirit caused havoc killing a person, who then went to the sky. Two cockatoos were also upset. The eyes of the evil spirit and the dead Aboriginal person are the Southern Cross and the white cockatoos are the Pointers.	Ecological laws		Reed 1965:34–36

Night sky phenomena (European)	Aboriginal mythological representation	Association	Aboriginal group or place	Source
Morning Star (Venus) and other (undesignated) stars	The Morning Star is two young women, who tried to escape Roll-a-mano, the man of the sea. His flaming branch exploded into sparks when it hit the water. Sparks became the stars. Roll-a-mano made a home in the sky and changed the women into the Morning Star.		Pennefather River area, Queensland	Reed 1965:115–17 Roth 1984(5):8
Alpha and Beta Centauri	Two brothers are burnt to death while cooking an emu. Their distressed mother was turned into a curlew whose cry can still be heard at night.		Flinders Ranges, SA	Ellis 1991:15–18 Tunbridge 1988:110

Night sky phenomena (European)	Aboriginal mythological representation	Association	Aboriginal group or place	Source
Four (undesignated) stars in the Milky Way and a Dark Patch	Two men, while circumcising an initiate with a fire stick, sent the lad into shock, which kills him. In revenge an old woman (the boy's mother's father's sister) who lives in the Milky Way in the Dark Patch, kills the two men. The boy, his string cross (representing a star) and the two men join the old woman permanently in the Milky Way.	Initiation and rituals and circumcision	Walbiri, NT Pitjantjatjara, SA, NT Aranda, NT Karadjeri, WA West Kimberley, WA Roper River, NT Arnhem Land, NT	Meggitt 1966:128 Roheim (1934) in Meggitt 1966:128 Spencer & Gillen 1899:224 Piddington (1933) in Meggitt 1966:128 Worms (1950) in Meggitt 1966:128 Berndt(1951)in Meggitt 1966:128 Warner 1937:533, 540
Orion	Crocodile following a string-bark canoe eats the man in the middle of the canoe because the man is sick.		Gagadju, NT	Neidjie 1989:6

Night sky phenomena (European)	Aboriginal mythological representation	Association	Aboriginal group or place	Source
Southern Cross and Pointers (*Alpha* and *Beta Centauri*)	*Mirrabooka* is an ancestral hero. His eyes are the pointers and the Southern Cross are his hands and feet.		Stradbroke Is., Queensland	Noonuccal and Bancroft 1993:66–67
Coal Sack	*Wawi*, the rainbow serpent lives in the deep waterholes of the Darling River. He burrows into the bank. One of *Wawi's* ancestors lives in the dark patch, the Coal Sack in the Sky. *Wawi* can only be visited by a healer by way of a rainbow.		Wuradjeri Weilwan Wongaibon, NSW	Mathews 1905:81; Mathews nd.:40; Radcliffe-Brown 1930:342
"Waving dark shadow in the Milky Way"	The rainbow serpent Karia lives in the Milky Way (as a dark patch).	Associated with the Bora grounds	Kamilaroi Yualarai Kwaimbal, NSW	Radcliffe-Brown 1930:344
Southern Cross	Two ancestral spirits who are also brothers are the Southern Cross.		Victorian groups	Isaacs 1980:151
Moon, planet Mars and other (undesignated) small stars	Moon was a very wicked man who went about doing harm. He devoured Eagle (Mars), whose two wives retaliated by striking Moon down. They cut him open and released their husband.		Gippsland, Victoria	Smyth 1972:431–32

Night sky phenomena (European)	Aboriginal mythological representation	Association	Aboriginal group or place	Source
Castor (*Alpha Geminorum* and Pollux (*Beta Geminorum*), Capella (*Alpha Aurigae*) and the daytime heat phenomenon of the mirage	Castor and Pollux are two hunters, *Yurree* and *Wanjel*, who pursue and kill *Purra*, a kangaroo (Capella). The mirage is the fire on which *Purra* is cooked.		Boorong and Wotjobaluk, Victorian Mallee	Stanbridge (1857) in MacPherson 1881:72; Massola 1968:111
Berenice's Hair (Coma Berenices)	A tree with three principal branches has birds drinking at the junction of the tree.	Dry weather	Boorong Wotjobaluk, Vic.	Stanbridge (1857) in MacPherson 1881:72; Massola 1968:111
Vega (*Alpha Lyrae*)	Vega is *Neilloan*, a mallee-hen and ancestral spirit who shows the people when and how to find the eggs of the mallee-hen.	Availability of mallee-hen eggs	Boorong Wotjobaluk, Vic.	Stanbridge (1857) in MacPherson 1881:72; Massola 1968:11

Night sky phenomena (European)	Aboriginal mythological representation	Association	Aboriginal group or place	Source
Hydra	A great hunter, *Barrukill*, and his dog sit near a kangaroo-rat. *Barrukill* is holding a firestick.		Mara, Western Victoria	Dawson 1981:101; Massola 1968:111, 1971:45
The moon and stars in Canis Major	The moon (*Mityan*), a native cat, fell in love with the wives (stars in Canis Major) of another man. The husband fought *Mityan*, who lost and was driven off. He has been wandering ever since.		Wotjobaluk, Vic.	Massola 1968:106 Smyth 1972:433
Southern Cross, the Coal Sack and the Pointers (*Alpha* and *Veta Centauri*)	The Southern Cross is a tree which affords protection to *Bunya*, an opossum, who is pursued by *Tchingal*, an emu, represented by the Coal Sack. The Pointers are the two great hunters who kill the emu and their spears are stuck in the tree (the stars of the Southern Cross).		Boorong Wotjobaluk, Vic.	Stanbridge (1857) in MacPherson 1881:72; Massola 1968:106–8 Smyth 1972:433

Night sky phenomena (European)	Aboriginal mythological representation	Association	Aboriginal group or place	Source
Canopus (*Alpha Carinae*) and a small red star (probably *Epsilon Carinae*)	Canopus is *War*, the male crow, and the small red star is the female crow. *War* is the carrier of fire to Aboriginal people of the Mallee.	Origin of fire	Boorong Wotjobaluk, Vic.	Stanbridge (1857) in MacPherson 1881:72; Massola 1968:21–24, 109
Altair (*Alpha Aquilae*), the Northern Crown (*Corona Borealis*), Sirius (*Alpha Canis Majoris*) and Rigel (*Beta Orionis*)	Altair is *Totyarquil*, a hunter, the Northern Cross is his boomerang. Sirius and Rigel are the male and female eagle pair (respectively), known as *Warepil*.	Origin of Murray River	Boorong Wotjobaluk, Vic.	MacPherson 1881:74–75, 78; Massola 1968:24–27, 110–11
Southern Cross	Believed to be an emu.		Kurnai Ya-itma-thang, Victoria	Massola 1968:108

Night sky phenomena (European)	Aboriginal mythological representation	Association	Aboriginal group or place	Source
Altair (*Alpha Aquilae*), two (undesignated) stars in Sagittarius and Atares (*Alpha Scorpii*) Southern Cross	Altair is *Bunjil*, the great eaglehawk; the two men in Sagittarius are two of *Bunjil's* young men, *Tadjeri*, the brush-tailed possum and *Tarnung*, the gliding phalanger. Antares is *Balayang, Bunjil's* brother. Two stars of the Southern Cross represent *Yukope*, the green par-akeet and *Dantum*, the blue mountain parrot, another two of *Bunjil's* young men.		Kulin, Vic.	Massola 1968:40, 110 Massola 1968:108
Morning star	If you look at the morning star, you will suffer separation and divorce from your spouse.	Divorce	Adnyamatana, Flinders Ranges, SA	Tunbridge 1988:45
Magellanic Clouds	Two mates, after journeying together, make a fire which carried them, via a mountain, up to the sky where they keep an eye on people below.	Marriage laws	Flinders Ranges, SA	Tunbridge 1988:95

Night sky phenomena (European)	Aboriginal mythological representation	Association	Aboriginal group or place	Source
Altair (*Alpha Aquilae*) and the stars on either side, with Vega *Alpha Lyrae*) and the stars on either side and Delphinus	The Brothers' constellation. Vega is the elder brother and Altair, the younger. Other stars are the sticks they hold. This constellation is associated with the *Dogai*, a female bogey who is hunted down by *Bu* (Delphinus).	North-west monsoon	Torres Strait Islands	Haddon in Lawrie 1970:211; Rivers in Haddon 1912(4):220, 221, (5):12–16
Stars of Ursa Major, Arcturus (*Alpha Bootis*) and *Gamma Corona Borealis*	Constellation of *Baidam* (western Torres Strait Islands) or *Beizam* (eastern Torres Strait Islands) - concerns four girls who caught a shark and killed it. Together they dragged it across a reef and threw it into the sea.	Change in season	Torres Strait Islands	Lawrie 1970:321: Rivers in Haddon 1912(4):219–220, (6):271
Dark patches in the Milky Way	Crow took a paper-bark basket and a wild cat into the Milky Way (river).		North-western Arnhem Land, NT	Warner 1937:533

Night sky phenomena (European)	Aboriginal mythological representation	Association	Aboriginal group or place	Source
Southern Cross and Pointers (*Alpha* and *Beta Centauri*)	Friendly crocodile, *Yungalpia*, is the Southern Cross, and the Pointers are night birds, *Moonaminya* and *Yikawanga*, who make thunder and lightning. The stars are all the people, animals, birds and fish that have died.	Death	Arnhem Land, NT	Maymuru 1978
Southern Cross	The Cross is the foot of *Warragunna*, an eaglehawk. His foot was hurt by his nephews because he refused to share food hunted by all three of them.	Kinship laws and reciprocity	Ooldea region, SA	Ker Wilson 1977:52–54

Night sky phenomena (European)	Aboriginal mythological representation	Association	Aboriginal group or place	Source
Morning Star (Venus)	After a person dies, his or her spirit is carried over the sea in a spirit-canoe which travels early in the morning along the string of light that comes from *Barnambir*, the morning star. The spirit goes to an island beyond the sun-rise. When the spirit is well-established on the island (*Baralku*), it sends a message back to earth by the morning star, who in turn relays it on to the relatives in the form of a white bird. *Barnambir*, the morning star, lives in *Purelko*, the island where the spirits of the dead reside.	*Barnambir* is a shining light held in a mesh bag, tied to the island of *Baralku* by *Jari*, the string of light which holds the light down so it never goes high in the sky	North-east Arnhem Land, NT Millingimbi, NT North-western Arnhem Land, NT Djambarbingu, NT; Galbu, NT	Berndt 1952:63–64 Warner 1937:524–28 Berndt and Berndt 1977:315–16 Mountford 1976:93–96
The morning star (Venus) and the moon	These represent two brothers, the younger of whom becomes a woman, the morning star.	Origin story	Western Cape York, Qld	Isaacs 1980:148–49
Evening star (Venus) and the moon	*Gidegal*, the moon, helps men with love magic. Songs sung by the men make the evening star twinkle and remind women of their lovers.	Love magic	Lardil, Mornington Island, NT	Isaacs 1980:163–66; Roughsey 1971:82–84

Night sky phenomena (European)	Aboriginal mythological representation	Association	Aboriginal group or place	Source
Morning star (Venus) and small (undesignated) stars either side or Vega (*Alpha Lyrae*), Altair (*Alpha Aquilae*) and the Northern Crown (*Corona Borealis*)	*Mullian*, an eaglehawk, was a cannibal who hunted humans. Friends of the dead decided to burn him. His charred bones fell out of his nest and he went to live in the sky as *Mullian-ga*, the morning star. On one side of the morning star is his arm (a small star), the other was burnt off. The other star is his possum-wife, *Moodai*.	Origin story	New South Wales groups (stars differ with groups, same story and characters)	Isaacs 1980:154; Parker 1953:57–58; Smyth 1972:286
Mars and two (undesignated) star-clusters and a dark patch	*Waijungari* is a newly initiated man, still covered in red ochre from the ceremonies. Two wives of another man (*Nepele*), seduced *Waijungari*, *Nepele* burnt *Waijungariis* camp out. *Waijungari* with the two women on his spear, escaped to the sky, where the women are now stars and *Waijungari* is the red planet Mars. The dark patch is an emu.		Jaralde (Yaraldi), Lake Alexandrina, SA	Isaacs 1980:154–55; Berndt and Berndt 1993:229–30

Night sky phenomena (European)	Aboriginal mythological representation	Association	Aboriginal group or place	Source
Orion	Three related fishermen in a canoe and their totemically taboo kingfish.	Ecological law	North-east Arnhem Land, NT	Wells 1973:37–44
Shooting stars and the moon	*Puggareetya*, a woman, used to play tricks on Snake who threw her and the rock she had put him behind, into the sky, where the Sky Spirit kept them. The big rock (*Weenah Leah*) is the moon and reflects the sun and *Puggareetya* is a shooting star thrown regularly across the heavens.	Origin story	Plangermairrener, Tasmania	Everett in Noonuccal 1990:115–19
Castor (*Alpha Geminorum*) and Pollux (*Beta Geminorum*)	Caterpillars go to the sky-world to look for a cockatoo who has died. They return to the earth as beautiful butterflies.	Metamorphosis and death	Mandalbingu, NT	Rule and Goodman 1979:118–25

Night sky phenomena (European)	Aboriginal mythological representation	Association	Aboriginal group or place	Source
Castor (*Alpha Geminorum*) and Pollux (*Beta Geminorum*) and 'the stars above them'	Two men who came down and slept at the base of a hill, threw fire down and then went to the sky as Castor and Pollux. They revived some women who had been killed by a stingray, by placing stinging ants on their breasts. The women are above the men as stars	Origin of fire	Oyster Bay, Tasmania	Roth 1899:84–95
Sunset	Sunset is caused by women fighting amongst themselves after men have tricked them by turning into swans to steal the women's weapons. Blood stains the clouds.	Origin of flannel flowers and black swans	Western Australia	Parker 1986:21–29; Ellis 1991:27–30
Dark patches on the moon	The whirlwind carried away a disobedient girl and put her into the moon.		Mowangum, Kimberley, WA	Utemorrah et al. 1980:48
Sun	Sun is a woman, *Mamoura*.	Female turtle	Groote Eylandt, NT	Mountford 1956:481–82
Sun	Sun is a woman, *Walo*, who goes on an underground path every night.	Origin story	Yirrkala, NT	Mountford 1956:502

Night sky phenomena (European)	Aboriginal mythological representation	Association	Aboriginal group or place	Source
Sun	The kookaburra's call signals the lighting of the stick-fire caused originally by the yolk of an emu egg bursting into flame when an angry brolga had an argument.	Origin story	Groups in NSW and in the Murrumbidgee area, NSW	Roberts and Mountford 1974:16; Parker 1985:1–2
Sun	Sun is a woman.		Mudbara, Victoria River area, NT	Berndt and Berndt 1977:319
Sun	Sun is a woman, *Bila*, who, having eaten many sky people, came to earth to satisfy her hunger. The lizard-men resisted her and her dogs, and brought the sun under control.	Night and day	South Australian groups	Mountford 1976:85
Sun	Breaking of eggs over a bonfire to create light and warmth.	Origin of sun		Hadley 1983
Sun	Sun is a woman, *Gnowee*, who lived on earth when it was always dark. Her little boy got lost and now she looks for him always, carrying a bark torch.	Origin story	Wotjobaluk, Victoria	Massola 1968:16, 106
Sun	Smashing of emu's egg which unites with wood.	Origin story	Murray River area, NSW/Vic.	Massola 1968:106

Night sky phenomena (European)	Aboriginal mythological representation	Association	Aboriginal group or place	Source
Sun	Sun is a woman who ran away because her choice of marriage partner was not respected. Ancestor spirits lifted her to the sky where she uses her campfire to warn people below, letting her fire die right down at night.	Origin story Marriage laws	Central Victoria	Ellis 1991:61–63
Sun and moon	The Sun Woman and the Moon Man witnessed the killing of people by a single monolith from the sky, set in motion by a giant goanna from the sky-world.		Lake Macquarie, NSW	Threkeld (1892) in Turbet 1989:126
Moon and Evening Star (Venus)	An ancestral-man, who lived near the claypan of the moonlight, died and his body became a nautilus shell (moon).	Death	Millingimbi, NT	Berndt and Berndt 1977:313–14
	Venus (the evening star) is a spirit. The lotus flower and the waterlily are symbols of the evening star, held up by the spirit.	Lotus and waterlily flowers origin		

Night sky phenomena (European)	Aboriginal mythological representation	Association	Aboriginal group or place	Source
Moon	Moon is a man, *Gidja*.	Death, menstruation and child-bearing	Koko-Yalunyu, Bloomfield River, Qld	McConnell 1930:350; 1931–32:21
Moon	The moon is a man, *Jumauria*, his wife and three children are in the 'face' of the moon.	Tides	Groote Eylandt, NT	Mountford 1956:484
Moon	Moon is a man, *Alinda*.	Death	Millingimbi and Yirrkala, NT	Mountford 1956:488–91; 1958:493–95; 1976a:89–91
Sun and moon	Sun is a woman, and moon is a man, who is also the guardian of the sky-world.		Wuradjeri, NSW	Berndt and Berndt 1977:413
Sun, Moon, Venus, Orion and the Pleiades	Sun is a woman, *Alinga*, and the moon is a man, *Atninja*. Venus, the morning star, is a lone woman, *Ungamilia*. Orion is an emu and the Pleiades are women.	Origin of sun and moon and death	Aranda, NT	Spencer and Gillen 1966:498–99

Night sky phenomena (European)	Aboriginal mythological representation	Association	Aboriginal group or place	Source
Sun and moon	Sun is a woman, *Wuriupranala*, moon is a man, *Japara*. *Japara* killed his wife because she did not prevent their son drowning. *Japara* searches the sky-world for them both, constantly moving camp. The lines on him are reminders of his scars. *Japara* also fought with *Purukupali*, the Great Creator. When *Japara* re-appears, he proceeds to eat the flesh of mangrove crabs until he becomes full. He gets ill and dies each month. The silvery crescent is his skeleton, and earth shine is his spirit.	Origin of sun, moon (death) and discovery of fire	Tiwi, Bathurst and Melville Islands, NT Arnhem Land, NT	Roberts and Mountford 1974:48, 66, 100; Sims 1978:166–67 Ellis 1991:65–68
Moon	Moon is a man who broke incest (kinship) laws causing death.	Death	Wolmeri and Lunga, Kimberley, WA	Kaberry 1939:199–200
Moon		Overcoming death by returning to one's country	Gadadju, NT	Neidjie et al 1985:57–58

Night sky phenomena (European)	Aboriginal mythological representation	Association	Aboriginal group or place	Source
Moon	*Kalu*, a man terrified of the blackness of the night, became pale and round, so obsessed was he by his problem. He became the moon and rests on a boomerang on occasions.	Origin story	Wongyr, WA	Brennan in Noonuccal 1990:147–65
Moon	Moon was an old man, whose nephew resents him because of his insults. The nephew tricks the old man into going up a tree and into the sky.	Origin story	Bagundji, western NSW; Adnjamathanha, SA	Isaacs 1980 145–46
Moon	Moon Man and his sexuality.	Death	Yarralin, Victoria River	Rose 1992:104–5
Sun	The great ancestor-spirit grabbed the red feathers of the firetail bird and flew around so fast that the feathers became bright as they burned, singeing the ancestor-spirit's white cockatoo body.	Origin myth of sun and fire	Pydairrerme, Tasman Peninsula, Tasmania	Everett in Noonuccal 1990:137–42

Night sky phenomena (European)	Aboriginal mythological representation	Association	Aboriginal group or place	Source
Sun and Moon	Sun is a 'goddess' in love with moon, 'god'. *Bahloo* also takes the form of an emu who creates and protects babies and their mothers. *Bahloo* loves young women. One night while playing in the river with two young girls, he goes too far and they push him into the river where his light fades. Now he gets into the sky without anyone noticing for he is so thin and pale. He becomes fat and wicked until someone else teaches him a lesson. *Bahloo* has his dogs which are snakes and he takes them with him when he crosses a stream despite the fear and dislike of Aborigines.	Birth and twins Origin story Death	NSW groups	Reed 1965:130–32; Hadley 1983; Ramsay Smith 1930:69–71; Parker 1953:74–76
Sun	Sun is a woman wandering in search of her lost son	Origin	Kurnai, Victoria	Massola 1968:106
Moon	Moon was *Menyan*, who endeavoured to make men live forever by giving them a drink of magic water. The plan was frustrated by a bronze-wing pigeon.	Death	Kulin, Victoria	Massola 1968:106

Night sky phenomena (European)	Aboriginal mythological representation	Association	Aboriginal group or place	Source
The Moon and the Southern Cross	Moon is *Narran*, a famous hunter forever stalking an emu, the Southern Cross.		Kurnai, Gippsland, Vic.	Massola 1968.106
Sun and Moon	Both are female. Sun Woman camped with the spirits and slept with Red Kangaroo. He gave her a large red cloak which allows her to achieve the redness she needs for heat and warmth. The Moon Woman copulates freely and grows thin from doing so, until she becomes pregnant.	Waxing and waning of moon Pregnancy	Jaralde, SA	Berndt and Berndt 1993:232–33
Moon	Two sisters swam a channel to an island to escape their duties. For food, they caught a fish from the lake but it escaped from off the cooking fire into a tree and up into the sky. It grows smaller when it is eaten.	Origin story		Reed 1965:37–40

Night sky phenomena (European)	Aboriginal mythological representation	Association	Aboriginal group or place	Source
Moon	The Moon Man helps two brothers. He helps free the younger one from a bees' nest and receives help in return.	Origin story Reciprocity	Princess Charlotte Bay, Qld	Reed 1965:103–5 Roth 1984(5):7
Sun, Moon and Venus	Sun (*tirng*, meaning 'light') is female and the moon (*Meeheaarong kuurta-ruung*, meaning 'hip') is male. Venus is female and is the mother of the sun.	Origin story	Western Victoria	Dawson 1981:99
Sun	The sun is a human ancestor who was misunderstood so he returned in sorrow and became 'a god'.	Origin story	Murrumbidgee River, NSW	Peck 1933:55–65
Moon	A 'bunyip' captured a girl, but the girl's lover came to her rescue. He was able to withstand the power of the bunyip's gaze and with a spear blinded the bunyip. The bunyip eventually died, leaving his one eye in the sky as the moon.	Origin	Murray River area, Victoria/NSW	Peck 1933:65–69

Night sky phenomena (European)	Aboriginal mythological representation	Association	Aboriginal group or place	Source
Moon	Moon Man (*Vira*) was trying to punish his nephew for taking his food. He fell backwards off a stick ladder and burst open, leaving marks on his belly. He went to the sky when he was tricked into climbing high up a tree by his nephews.	Marks on the moon Origin story	Adnyamatana, Flinders Ranges	Tunbridge 1988:68–69
Sun, moon and darkness	All things can be divided: things of the sun, things of the moon and things of the night—'without-light'.	Separation of the three forms	Island of Duaun, Torres Strait (A similar myth exists among the Kiwai Papuans)	Lawrie 1970:132–34
Moon	The moon, *Carcurrah*, fell to earth because he became dizzy. Some say he was pushed back up by the growing grass, others say he sank through the earth and came out the other side. The moon, feeling deserted, cursed the animals, condemning them to a mortal life.	Death	Tully River area, Queensland	Henry 1967:34, 38
Moon	Moon and parrot fish debate mortality.	Death	North-western Arnhem Land, NT	Warner 1937:523–24

Night sky phenomena (European)	Aboriginal mythological representation	Association	Aboriginal group or place	Source
Moon and Sun(s)	The moon is the husband of the sun(s). At new moon, he is starving and so sets off on a fishing expedition. He is always successful and his belly (at full moon) is gorged. His wife, the suns (there are two), always travelling westwards in search of green ants. The suns are sisters: in the cold season, it is the elder who visits, and in the hot season, it is the younger.	Origin story	Cape Bedford area, Queensland	Roth 1984(5):7
Moon	The earthworm sends moon up into the sky regularly every month to remind people of his skill as a healer (he had, in the past, bored a hole into the diseased part of a turkey ancestor's foot and sucked out the putrid matter, curing him). The moon is a mother of the earthworm and, like him, bores his way out of the ground, rises up on high, sinks once more and dies. As he has plenty of brothers, he sends along a different one every month.	Healing and death	Boulia district, Queensland The Tully River people (Queensland) also believe there is a different moon every month	Roth 1984(5):7

Night sky phenomena (European)	Aboriginal mythological representation	Association	Aboriginal group or place	Source
Moon and two (undesignated) stars nearby	The moon has two wives. When the moon was about to cook himself some shells, having no tree-bark at hand, he divested himself of his skin and used it instead of bark to wrap up the sheets. But with his skin off, there was no light which angered the bats (his children) who beat him up and threw him into the sea. Now he covers himself with charcoal so he cannot be seen and speared. Only his face is visible which he covers with white pipe-clay.	Name for pipe-clay (aro-a) is the name given to the moon	Pennefather River area, Queensland	Roth 1984(5):7

Appendix 2: The 88 Constellations

Latin Name	Genitive	English Name	Brightest Stars (mentioned in the text)	Apparent Magnitude
Andromeda	Andromedae	Andromeda		
Antlia	Antliae	Air Pump		
Apus	Apodis	Bird of Paradise or Bee		
Aquarius	Acquarii	Water Carrier		
Aquila	Aquilae	Eagle	Altair	0.8
Ara	Arae	Altar		
Aries	Arietis	Ram		
Auriga	Aurigae	Charioteer	Capella (multiple star)	0.1
Boötes	Boötis	Bear Driver or Herdsman	Arcturus	-0.1
Caelum	Caeli	Graving Tool		
Camelopardalis	Camelopardalis	Giraffe		

Latin Name	Genitive	English Name	Brightest Stars (mentioned in the text)	Apparent Magnitude
Cancer	Cancri	Crab		
Canes Venatici	Canum Venaticorum	Hunting Dogs		
Canis Major	Canis Majoris	Larger Dog	Sirius (multiple star)	-1.5
Canis Minor	Canis Minoris	Smaller Dog	Procyon (multiple star)	0.3
Capricornus	Capricorni	Sea Goat		
Carina	Carinae	Keel	Canopus	-0.7
Cassiopeia	Cassiopeiae	Cassiopeia		
Centaurus	Centauri	Centaur	Alpha and Beta Centauri (multiple stars)	-0.3, 0.6
Cepheus	Cephei	Cepheus		
Cetus	Ceti	Whale		
Chamaeleon	Chamaeleontis	Chameleon		
Circinus	Circini	Compasses		

Latin Name	Genitive	English Name	Brightest Stars (mentioned in the text)	Apparent Magnitude
Columba	Columbae	Dove		
Coma Berenices	Comae Berenices	Berenice's Hair		
Corona Australis	Coronae Australis	Southern Crown		
Corona Borealis	Coronae Borealis	Northern Crown		
Corvus	Corvi	Crow		
Crater	Crateris	Cup		
Crux Australis	Crucis	Southern Cross	Acrux, Beta Crucis	0.9, 1.3
Cygnus	Cygni	Swan	Deneb	1.3
Delphinus	Delphini	Dolphin		
Dorado	Doradus	Goldfish or Swordfish		
Draco	Draconis	Dragon		
Equuleus	Equulei	Little Horse		
Eridanus	Eridani	River	Achernar	0.5
Fornax	Fornacis	Furnace		

Latin Name	Genitive	English Name	Brightest Stars (mentioned in the text)	Apparent Magnitude
Gemini	Geminorum	Twins	Pollux and Castor	1.2, 1.6
Grus	Gruis	Crane		
Hercules	Herculis	Hercules		
Horologium	Horologii	Clock		
Hydra	Hydrae	Water Snake		
Hydrus	Hydri	Sea Serpent		
Indus	Indi	Indian		
Lacerta	Lacertae	Lizard		
Leo	Leonis	Lion	Regulus (multiple star)	1.3
Leo Minor	Leonis Minoris	Smaller Lion		
Lepus	Leporis	Hare		
Libra	Librae	Scales		
Lupus	Lupi	Wolf		

Latin Name	Genitive	English Name	Brightest Stars (mentioned in the text)	Apparent Magnitude
Lynx	Lyncis	Lynx		
Lyra	Lyrae	Lyre	Vega	0.0
Mensa	Mensae	Table (Mountain)		
Microscopium	Microscopii	Microscope		
Monoceros	Monocerotis	Unicorn		
Musca	Muscae	Fly		
Norma	Normae	Level		
Octans	Octantis	Octant		
Ophiuchus	Ophiuchi	Serpent-Bearer		
Orion	Orionis	Orion	Rigel, Betelgeuse, Bellatrix (multiple and variable stars)	0.1, 0.8, 1.6
Pavo	Pavonis	Peacock		
Pegasus	Pegasi	Pegasus, the Flying Horse		

Latin Name	Genitive	English Name	Brightest Stars (mentioned in the text)	Apparent Magnitude
Perseus	Persei	Perseus		
Phoenix	Phoenicis	Phoenix		
Pictor	Pictoris	Easel or Painter		
Pisces	Piscium	Fishes		
Piscis Austrinus	Piscis Austrini	Southern Fish	Formalhaut	1.2
Puppis	Puppis	Stern or Poop		
Pyxis	Pyxidis	Mariner's Compass		
Reticulum	Reticuli	Net		
Sagitta	Sagittae	Arrow		
Sagittarius	Sagittarii	Archer		
Scorpius	Scorpii	Scorpion	Antares (multiple and variable stars)	1.0
Sculptor	Sculptoris	Sculptor		
Scutum	Scuti	Shield		

Latin Name	Genitive	English Name	Brightest Stars (mentioned in the text)	Apparent Magnitude
Serpens	Serpentis	Serpent		
Sextans	Sextantis	Sextant		
Taurus	Tauri	Bull	Aldebaran (multiple star)	0.8
Telescopium	Telescopii	Telescope		
Triangulum	Trianguli	Triangle		
Triangulum Australe	Trianguli Australis	Southern Triangle		
Tucana	Tucanae	Toucan		
Ursa Major	Ursae Majoris	Great Bear		
Ursa Minor	Ursae Minoris	Little Bear		
Vela	Velorum	Sails		
Virgo	Virginis	Virgin	Spica (variable star)	1.0
Volans	Volantis	Flying Fish		
Vulpecula	Vulpeculae	Fox		

Appendix 3: Star Magnitudes

Magnitude is concerned with a star's apparent brightness, not its real luminosity. The scale works so that the more brilliant the star, the lower its magnitude. Thus the very bright stars are of magnitude 1, magnitude 2 is fainter, magnitude 3 is fainter still. Stars below magnitude 6 are usually invisible to the naked eye even on a very dark night. The measurements of magnitude have been devised according to a logarithmic scale. Thus a star of magnitude 1.0 is exactly a hundred times as bright as a star of magnitude 6.0.

Magnitudes, starting from zero, are roughly as follows:

0: Extremely bright stars such as Capella in Auriga and Vega in Lyra.

1: Very bright stars standing out against their neighbours. Conventionally, any star brighter than magnitude 1.5 is said to be 'first magnitude'. There are only 21 of them.

2: Moderately bright stars.

3: Fainter stars able to be seen in conditions of moonlight or mist.

4: Very faint stars that can be concealed by moonlight.

5: Stars too faint to be seen unless the sky is dark and clear.

6: Faintest stars visible with the naked eye only under extremely good viewing conditions.

Venus, the morning and evening star, and the most brilliant of the planets have a magnitude of -4. There are only four stars with magnitudes below zero: Sirus (-1.4), Canopus (-0.7), Alpha Centauri (-0.3) and Arcturus (-0.4). On this scale, the Sun's magnitude is almost -27.

Appendix 4: Australian Aboriginal Groups and Communities mentioned in the text[1]

Adnyamatana	SA
Alawa	NT
Andagarinja	SA
Anmatjara	NT
Anula	NT
Arabana	SA
Aranda	NT
Bagundji	NSW
Bibbulmun	WA
Booandik	SA
Boorong	Vic
Dharamba	NSW
Dieri	NT
Djambarbingu	NT
Djara	WA
Djauan	NT
Gagadju	NT
Galbu	NT
Gullibul	NSW
Gundungurra	NSW
Gunwinggu	NT

---

1 There are many alternate spellings throughout the literature

Jajauring	NSW
Jaralde (Yaraldi)	SA
Jupagalk	NSW
Kamilaroi	NSW
Karadjeri	WA
Karruru	SA
Koko-yalunyu	Qld
Kukatja (Gugadja)	WA
Kulin	Vic
Kurnai	Vic
Kuurn kopan noot	Vic
Kwadju	Qld
Kwaimbal	NSW
Lardil	NT
Lunga	WA
Luritja (Loritja)	NT
Mandalbingu	NT
Mara	Vic
Meenamatta	SA
Meriam	Qld
Moil	NT
Moporr	Vic
Mowanjum	WA
Mudbara	NT
Mukjarawaint	Vic

Murinbata	NT
Needwonee	Tas
Ngadadjara	WA
Ngadjuri	SA
Ngalia	NT
Ngeumba	NSW
Ngulugwongga	NT
Njangomada	WA
Nyoongah	WA
Nyulnyul	WA
Pilbara	WA
Pintupi (Pintubi)	NT
Pirt kopan noot	Vic
Pitjantjatjara	NT/SA
Plangermairrener	Tas
Pydurrerme	Tas
Tiwi	NT
Wailwun	NSW
Walbiri	NT
Wandandia	NSW
Wiilman	WA
Wolmeri	WA
Wongaibon	NSW
Wongyr	WA
Wotjabaluk	Vic

Night Skies of Aboriginal Australia

Wumbaio	NSW
Wuradjeri	NSW
Ya itma thang	Vic
Yaoro	WA
Yarra	Vic
Yarralin	NT
Yolngu	NT
Yualarai	NSW

Bibliography

Allen, Richard Hinckley (1963), *Star names: their lore and meaning*, Dover Publications, New York (first published 1899).

Altman, J.C. (1991), Hunter-gatherer subsistence production in Arnhem land: the original affluence hypothesis re-examined, in W.H. Edwards, *Traditional Aboriginal Society: a reader*, Macmillan, South Melbourne, Crows Nest (first published 1984).

Austin-Broos, Diane (1994), Narratives of the encounter at Ntaria, *Oceania* 65(2).

Australian Broadcasting Commission (ABC) and Discovery Productions (1993), *The big wet*, (Executive Producer Diane Gilmour), Natural History Unit, Melbourne.

Barnes, B. (1973), The comparison of belief-systems: anomaly versus falsehood, in R. Horton and R. Finnegan (eds), *Modes of thought*, Faber and Faber, London.

Bates, Daisy (P.J. Bridge ed.) (1992), *Aboriginal Perth Bibbulmun biographies and legends*, Hesperian, Victoria Park, WA.

Beale, Bob (1994), Alice to Somewhere, in *The Sydney Morning Herald*, 12 May 1994.

Beattie, J. (1966), Ritual and social change, *Man* (N S) 1.

Berlin, Brent, Dennis E. Breedlove and Peter H. Raven (1973), General principles of classification and nomenclature in folk biology, *American Anthropologist* 75.

Berlin, Brent and Paul Kay (1971) *Basic color terms: their universality and evolution*, University of California Press, Berkeley.

Berndt, Catherine H. (1988), Traditional Aboriginal oral literature, in Jack Davis and Bob Hodge (eds) *Aboriginal writing today*, Australian Institute of Aboriginal Studies, Canberra.

Berndt, Catherine and Raymond Meeks (1988), *When the world was new in Rainbow Snakeland*, Horowitz Grahame in association with Ashton Scholastic, Gosford.

Berndt, Ronald M. (1941), Tribal migrations and myths centring on Ooldea, South Australia, *Oceania* 12(1).

Berndt, Ronald M. (1946–7), Wuradjeri magic and "clever men", *Oceania*, 17(4), 18(1).

Berndt, Ronald M. (1952), *Djanggawul: an Aboriginal religious cult of north eastern Arnhem Land*, Routledge and Kegan Paul, London.

Berndt, R.M. and C.H. Berndt (1951), *Sexual behaviour in western Arnhem Land*, Viking Fund, New York.

Berndt, Ronald M. (1959), The concept of "the tribe" in the western desert of Australia, *Oceania*, 30(2).

Berndt, R.M. and C.H. Berndt (1970), *Man, land and myth in north Australia: the Gunwinggu people*, Ure Smith, Sydney.

Berndt, R.M. and C.H. Berndt (1974), *The first Australians*, Ure Smith, Sydney (first printed 1952).

Berndt, R.M. and C.H. Berndt (1977), *The world of the first Australians*, Ure Smith, Sydney.

Berndt, R.M. and C.H. Berndt (1989), *The speaking land: Myth and story in Aboriginal Australia*, Penguin Books, Ringwood.

Berndt, Ronald M. and Catherine H. Berndt, with John E. Stanton (1993), *A world that was, The Yaraldi of the Murray River and the Lakes, South Australia*, Melbourne University Press, Melbourne.

Bhathal, Ragbir and Graeme White (1991), *Under the Southern Cross: a brief history of astronomy in Australia*, Kangaroo Press, Kenthurst.

Blainey, Geoffrey (1975), *Triumph of the nomads: a history of ancient Australians*, Macmillan, South Melbourne.

Bozic, S. and A. Marshall (1972), *Aboriginal myths*, Gold Star Publications, Melbourne.

Buchanan, Uncle Harry (1992), *Gumbaynggir yuludarra*, Vol. 1, Gumbaynggir Language and Culture group.

Buckley, R. et al (1968), Group project on Andagarinja women, Vol. 2, University of Adelaide, Adelaide.

Bulmer, Ralph (1967), Why is the cassowary not a bird? A problem of zoological classification among the Karam of the New Guinea Highlands, *Man* (2)1.

Cairns, H.C. and D.F. Branagan (1992), Artificial patterns on rock surfaces in the Sydney region, New South Wales: evidence for Aboriginal time charts and sky maps, in J. Macdonald and I. Haskovic (eds) *State of the art: regional art studies in Australia and Melanesia*, Australian Rock Art Research Association, Melbourne.

Cairns, Hugh (1993), Aboriginal sky-mapping? Possible astronomical interpretations of Australian Aboriginal ethnographic and archaeological material in Clive L.N. Ruggles (ed.), *Archaeoastronomy in the 1990s*, Group D Publications Ltd, Loughborough, UK (kindly shown to author by John Clegg).

Cawte, John (1974), *Medicine is the law: studies in psychiatric anthropology in Australian tribal societies*, University Press of Hawaii, Honululu.

Charles, Mary (1993), *Why the emu cannot fly*, Magabala Books Aboriginal Corporation, Broome.

Chase, A. and P. Sutton (1991), Australian Aborigines in a rich environment in W.H. Edwards *Traditional Aboriginal society: a reader*, Macmillan, South Melbourne, Crows Nest (first published 1981).

Conklin, Harold (1955), Hanunoo Color categories *Southwestern Journal of Anthropology* 11(4).

Dawson, James (1981), *Australian Aborigines: the languages and customs of several tribes of Aborigines in the western district of Victoria, Australia*, Australian Institute of Aboriginal Studies, Canberra (first published 1881).

Dean, John (1979), Controversy over classification: a case study from the history of botany in Barry Barnes and Steven Shapin (1979), *Natural order, historical studies of scientific culture*, Sage Publications, Beverly Hills, London.

Diamond, J. (1966), Zoological classification systems of a primitive people, *Science* 151.

Douglas, M. (1966), *Purity and danger, an analysis of concepts of pollution and taboo*, Routledge and Kegan Paul, London.

Douglas, M. (1975), *Implicit meanings: essays in anthropology*, Routledge and Kegan Paul, London.

Durack, Mary (1969), *The rock and the sand*, Constable, London.

Durkheim, Emile and Marcel Mauss (1970), *Primitive classification*, Cohen and West, London (first published 1903).

Eliade, M. (1960), *Myths, dreams and mysteries*, Harvill Press, London.

Eliade, M. (1973), *Australian religions: an introduction*, Cornell University Press, Ithaca.

Elkin, A.P. (1930), The Rainbow Serpent: myth in north-west Australia, *Oceania* 1(3).

Elkin, A.P. (1945), *Aboriginal men of high degree*, Australian Publishing, Sydney.

Elkin, A.P. (1974), *The Australian Aborigines*, Angus and Robertson, Sydney (first published 1938).

Ellis, Jean A. (1991), *From a dreamtime: Australian Aboriginal legends*, Collins Dover, Victoria.

Firth, R. (1952), *Elements of social organisation*, Watts, London.

Frake, Charles O. (1961), The diagnosis of disease among the Subanum of Mindanao, *American Anthropologist* 63(1).

Goodenough, Ward H. (1957), Cultural anthropology and linguistics, *Monograph series on language and linguistics* No 9, Georgetown University, Georgetown.

Green, Gracie and Joe Tramacchi and Lucille Gill (1993), *Tjarany Roughtail The dreaming of the roughtail lizard and other stories*, Magabala Books, Broome.

Gunson, N. (1974), *Aboriginal reminscences and papers of L.E. Threkeld*, Australian Institute of Aboriginal Studies, Canberra.

Haddon, A.C. et al (1912), *Reports of the Cambridge anthropological expedition to Torres Straits*, Vols 4, 5, 6 Cambridge University Press, Cambridge.

Hadley, Eric and Tessa (1983), *Legends of the sun and moon*, Cambridge University Press, Cambridge.

Harney, W.E. and A.P. Elkin (1949), *Songs of the songmen: Aboriginal myths retold*, F.W. Cheshire, Melbourne and London.

Harrison, Edward (1985), *Masks of the universe*, Macmillan and Collier Macmillan, New York, London.

Hassell, E. (1934–5), Myths and folktales of the Wheelman Tribe of south-western Australia, *Folklore*, 46.

Haynes, Rosslynn D. (1992), Aboriginal astronomy, *Australian journal of astronomy*, 4 (3).

Henry, C.J. (1967), *Girroo Gurrll: the first surveyor and other Aboriginal legends*, Smith and Paterson, Brisbane.

Hiatt, L.R. (1971), Secret pseudo-procreation rites among the Australian Aborigines in L.R. Hiatt and C. Jayawardena (eds) *Anthropology in Oceania: essays presented to Ian Hogbin*, Angus and Robertson, Sydney.

Hiatt, L.R. (1975), Introduction in L.R. Hiatt (ed.) *Australian Aboriginal mythology*, Australian Institute of Aboriginal Studies, Canberra.

Horton, R. (1971), African traditional thought and western science in M.F.D. Young (ed.), *Knowledge and control: new directions for the sociology of education*, Collier-Macmillan, London.

Howitt, A.W. (1904), *The native tribes of south-east Australia*, Macmillan, London.

Isaacs, Jennifer (1980), *Australian Dreaming: 40,000 years of Aboriginal history*, Landsdowne Press, Sydney.

Jaki, Stanley L. (1973), *The Milky Way: an elusive road for science*, Science History Publications David and Charles, Devon.

Kaberry, P.M. (1939), *Aboriginal women: sacred and profane*, Routledge, London.

Ker Wilson, Barbara (1977), *Tales told to Kabbarli: Aboriginal legends collected by Daisy Bates*, Angus and Robertson, London, Sydney, Melbourne (first published 1972).

Landtman, Gunnar (1917), *The folk-tales of the Kiwai Papuans*, Printing Office, Finnish Society of Literature, Helingsfors.

Lawrie, M. (1970), *Myths and legends of Torres Strait*, University of Queensland Press, St Lucia.

Lévi-Strauss, C. (1967), *The savage mind*, Weidenfeld and Nicolson, London.

Lévi-Strauss, C. (1967), The story of Asdiwal in E. Leach (ed.) *The structural study of myth and totemism*, Tavistock, London.

Lewis, David (1976), Observations on route finding among the Aboriginal people of the western desert region of central Australia, *Oceania* 46 (4).

Lounsbury, Floyd G. (1964), The formal analysis of Crow- and Omaha-type kinship terminologies, in W.E. Goodenough (ed.), *Explorations in Cultural anthropology*, McGraw Hill, New York.

Lowe, Pat and Jimmy Pike (1990), *Jilji life in the Great Sandy Desert*, Magabala Books, Broome.

Lucich, Peter (1969), *Childrens stories from the Worora Australia*, Australian Institute of Aboriginal studies, Canberra.

Mabo and Others V the State of Queensland and the Commonwealth of Australia in the High Court of Australia (3 June 1992), Judgement per Brennan J 66 Australian Law Journal Reports.

McConnel, Ursula (1930), The Rainbow Serpent in North Queensland, *Oceania* 1 (3).

McConnel, Ursula (1931–2), A moon legend from the Bloomfield River, North Queensland *Oceania* 2.

McConnel, Ursula (1957), *Myths of the Munkan*, Melbourne University Press, Carlton.

MacPherson, Peter (1881), Astronomy of the Australian Aborigines, *Journal and proceedings of the Royal Society of NSW* Vol 15.

Maddock, Kenneth (1974), *The Australian Aborigines: a portrait of their society*, Penguin, Ringwood (first published 1972).

Maddock, Kenneth (1975), The emu anomaly in L.R. Hiatt (ed.) *Australian Aboriginal mythology*, Australian Institute of Aboriginal Studies, Canberra.

Maegraith, B.G. (1932), The astronomy of the Aranda and Loritja tribes, Adelaide University Field Anthropology No 10, *Transactions of the Royal Society of South Australia* Vol 56.

Manning, J. (1882) Notes on the Aborigines of New Holland *Journal and proceedings of the Royal Society of New South Wales* 16.

Massola, Aldo (1968), *Bunjils cave myths: legends and superstitions of the Aborigines of south-east Australia*, Landsdowne, Melbourne.

Massolo, William Aldo (1971), *The Aborigines of south eastern Australia as they were*, Heinemann, Melbourne.

Mathews, Janet (1982), *The two worlds of Jimmy Barker*, Australian Institute of Aboriginal Studies, Canberra.

Mathews, Janet (1994), *The opal that turned into fire*, Magabala Books Aboriginal Corporation, Broome.

Mathews, R.H. (1899), *Folklore of the Australian Aborigines*, Hennessey, Harper and Company, Sydney.

Mathews, R.H. (1905), *Ethnological notes on the Aboriginal tribes of New South Wales and Victoria*, F.W. White, Sydney.

Mathews, R.H. (n.d.), *Unpublished notebooks*, 3 and 4 (kindly loaned to the author by Jim Smith).

Maymuru, Narritjan (1978), *The Milky Way*, Harcourt Brace Jovanovich Group, Sydney, Melbourne.

Meggitt, M.J. (1966), Gadjari among the Walbiri Aborigines of central Australia, *Oceania Monograph* No 14, University of Sydney Press, Sydney.

Meyer, H.E.A. (1946), *Manners and customs of the Encounter Bay tribe South Australia*, George Dehane for Government, Adelaide.

Montagu, Ashley (1974), *Coming into being among the Australian Aborigines: the procreation beliefs of the native tribes of Australia*, Routledge and Kegan Paul, London (first edition 1937).

Morgan, Sally (1992), *The flying emu and other Australian stories*, Viking Penguin, Ringwood.

Morphy, Howard (1991), Ancestral connections, *Art and an Aboriginal system of knowledge*, University of Chicago Press, Chicago.

Mountford, Charles, P. (1937), Aboriginal crayon drawings from the Warburton Ranges in Western Australia relating to the wanderings of two ancestral beings in Wati Kutjara, *South Australian Museum records*, 6.

Mountford, Charles, P. (1938), Aboriginal crayon drawings 3: The Legend of Wati Jula and the Kunkarun Women *Transactions of the Royal Society of South Australia* 62(2).

Mountford, Charles, P. (1939), An Anyamatana legend of the Pleiades, *Victorian Naturalist*, Vol 56.

Mountford, Charles, P. (1948), *Brown men and red sand journeyings in wild Australia*, Angus and Robertson, Sydney.

Mountford, Charles, P. (1956), Arnhem Land: art, myth and symbolism in *Records of the American-Australian scientific expedition to Arnhem Land*, Vol 1, Melbourne University Press, Melbourne.

Mountford, Charles, P. (1976a), *Before time began: legends of the Dreamtime*, Thomas Nelson, West Melbourne.

Mountford, Charles, P. (1976b), *Nomads of the Australian desert*, Rigby, Adelaide.

Neidjie, Bill et al (1985), *Kakadu man ... Bill Neidjie*, Mybrood NSW.

Neidje, Bill (1989), *Story about feeling*, Magabala Books, Broome.

Nilsson, Martin P. (1920), *Primitive time-reckoning*, G.W.K. Gleerup, Lund.

Noonuccal, Oodgeroo (1990), *Legends and landscapes*, Random House, Milsons Point.

Noonuccal, Oodgeroo and Bronwyn Bancroft (1993), *Stradbroke Dreamtime*, Angus and Robertson, Pymble.

O'Brien, May L. (1990), *The legend of the seven sisters: a traditional story from Western Australia*, Aboriginal Studies Press, Canberra.

Parker, K. Langloh (1953), *Australian legendary tales: Noongay-burrahs as told to the piccannies*, Angus and Robertson, Sydney (first published 1896).

Parker, K. Langloh (1985), *Tales of the Dreamtime*, Angus and Robertson, London, Sydney, Melbourne (first published 1975).

Peck, C.W. (1925), *Australian legends*, Parts 1 and 2, Stafford, Sydney.

Peck, C.W. (1933), *Australian legends*, Lothian, Melbourne.

Piddington, Ralph (1930), The Water Serpent in Karadjeri mythology, *Oceania* 1(3).

Piddington, Ralph (1932), The totemic system of the Karadjeri tribe, *Oceania* 1(4).

Plomley N.J.B. (1966), *Friendly mission*, Tasmanian Historical Research Association, Hobart.

Radcliffe-Brown, A.R. (1930), The Rainbow Serpent Myth in south-east Australia, *Oceania* (3).

Ramsay Smith, W. (1930), *Myths and legends of the Australian Aboriginals*, George G. Harrap, London, Bombay, Sydney.

Raymo, Chet (1985), *The soul of the night sky, an astronomical pilgrimage*, Prentice-Hall Inc., New Jersey.

Raymo, Chet (1986), Comet Halley: an appreciation, *Sky and telescope*, July 1986.

Reed, A.W. (1965), *Aboriginal fables and legendary tales*, A.H. and A.W. Reed, Sydney, Wellington, Auckland.

Reid, Janice (1986), *Sorcerers and healing spirits: continuity and change in an Aboriginal medical system*, Australian National University Press (Pergamon Press), Canberra.

Reynolds, Henry (1983), *The other side of the frontier: Aboriginal resistance to the European invasion of Australia*, Penguin, Ringwood (first published 1981).

Ridley, W. (1875), *Kamilaroi and other Australian languages*, Government Printer, Sydney.

Roberts, Ainslie and Charles P Mountford (1974), *The Dreamtime book: Australian Aboriginal myths*, Rigby, Adelaide, Sydney (first published in 1973).

Robinson, Roland (1965), *The man who sold his Dreaming*, Currawong, Sydney.

Robinson, Roland (1966), *Aboriginal myths and legends*, Sun Books, Melbourne.

Robinson, Roland (1967), *Legend and Dreaming*, Edwards and Shaw, Sydney (first published 1952).

Roe, Paddy and Stephen Muecke (1983), *Gularabulu stories from the west Kimberley*, Fremantle Arts Centre Press, Fremantle.

Roheim, G. (1925), *Australian totemism: a psychoanalytic study in anthropology*, Allen and Unwin, London.

Roheim, G. (1945), *The eternal ones of the dream: a psychoanalytic interpretation of Australian myth and ritual*, International Universities Press, New York.

Rose, Deborah Bird (1992), *Dingo makes us human: life and land in an Australian Aboriginal culture*, Cambridge University Press, Cambridge.

Roth, H. Ling (1899), *The Aborigines of Tasmania*, F. King and Sons, Halifax (first published 1890).

Roth, W.E. (1984), *The Queensland Aborigines*, Vol II, Hesperian Press, Victoria Park W.A. (first published 1901).

Roughsey, Dick (Goobalathaldin) (1971), *Moon and rainbow: an autobiography of an Aboriginal*, A.H. and A.W. Reed, Sydney.

Rule, Hugh and Stuart Goodman (eds) (1979), *Gulpilils stories of the Dreamtime*, William Collins, Sydney.

Sahlins, Marshall (1972), *Stone age economics*, Tavistock, London.

Shapin, Steven (1979), Homo Phrenologicus: anthropological perspectives on an historical problem in Barry Barnes and Steven Shapin (1979), *Natural order, historical studies of scientific culture*, Sage Publications, Beverley Hills, London.

Sharp, Nonie (1993), *Stars of Tagai: the Torres Strait Islanders*, Aboriginal Studies Press, Canberra.

Sharp, Nonie (1994), *Malos law in court: the religious background to the Mabo case*, The Charles Strong Memorial Trust, Adelaide (kindly shown to author by Friedegard Tomasetti).

Sims, Michael (1978), Tiwi Cosmology in L.R. Hiatt (ed.) *Australian Aboriginal concepts*, Australian Institute of Aboriginal Studies, Canberra.

Smith, Jim (1992), *Aboriginal legends of the Blue Mountains*, Jim Smith, Wentworth Falls.

Smith, Mrs James (1880), *The Booandik tribe of South Australian Aborigines: A sketch of their habits, customs and language*, E. Spiller, Government Printer, Adelaide.

Smyth, R. Brough (1878), *The Aborigines of Victoria*, Government Printer, Melbourne.

Smyth, R. Brough (1972), *The Aborigines of Victoria*, Vol. 2, John Currey, O'Neil, Melbourne (first published 1876).

Spencer, Baldwin and F.J. Gillen (1899), *The native tribes of central Australia*, Macmillan, London.

Spencer, Baldwin and F.J. Gillen (1966), *The Arunta: a study of stone age people*, Anthropological publications, Oosterhout NB, The Netherlands.

Stanbury, Peter and John Clegg (1990), *A field guide to Aboriginal rock engravings*, Sydney University Press, Sydney.

Stanner, W.E.H. (1991), The Dreaming in W.H. Edwards (ed.), *Traditional Aboriginal society: a reader*, Macmillan, South Melbourne, Crows Nest (first published 1956).

Stanner, W.E.H. (1959–63), On Aboriginal religion, *Oceania Monograph No 11*, University of Sydney, Sydney.

Stanner, W.E.H. (1965), Religion, totemism and symbolism in R.M. and C.H. Berndt (eds) *Aboriginal man in Australia*, Angus and Robertson, Sydney.

Strehlow T.G.H. (1907 unpublished English translation), *The Aranda and Loritja tribes of central Australia*, Part 1, Municipal Ethnological Museum, Joseph Baer and Co, Translation by Hans D Oberscheidt, (kindly shown to author by Professor Diane Austin-Broos).

Strehlow T.G.H. (1968), *Aranda traditions*, Melbourne University Press, Melbourne (first published 1947).

Sutton, Peter (1988), Myth as history, history as myth in Ian Keen (ed.), *Being black: Aboriginal cultures in settled Australia*, Aboriginal Studies Press, Canberra.

Tindale, N.B. (1936), Legend of the Wati Kutjara, Warburton Range, Western Australia, *Oceania* 7(2).

Tindale, N.B. (1938), Prupe and Koromararange: a legend of the Tanganekald, Coorong, South Australia *Royal Society of South Australian transactions*, 62.

Tindale, N.B. (1959), Totemic Beliefs in the Western Desert of Australia Part 1: Women who became the Pleiades, *Records of the South Australian Museum* 13(3).

Tindale, Norman B. (1974), *Aboriginal tribes of Australia*, Australian University Press, Canberra.

Tindale, Norman B. (1978), Notes on a few Australian Aboriginal concepts in L.R. Hiatt (ed.) *Australian Aboriginal concepts*, Australian Institute of Aboriginal studies, Canberra.

Tunbridge, Dorothy (1988), *Flinders Ranges Dreaming*, Australian Studies Press, Canberra.

Turbet, Peter (1989), *The Aborigines of the Sydney District Before 1788*, Kangaroo Press, Kenthurst.

Tyler, Stephen A (1969), *Cognitive Anthropology*, Holt, Rinehart and Winston Inc, New York.

Utemorrah, Daisy et al (1980), *Visions of Mowanjum: Aboriginal writings from the Kimberley*, Rigby, Adelaide.

von Brandenstein, C.G. and A.P. Thomas (1975), *Taruru Aboriginal song poetry from the Pilbara*, University Press of Hawaii, Honululu.

Warlukurlangu Artists (1987), *Yuendumu Doors, Kuruwarri*, Australian Institute of Aboriginal Studies, Canberra.

Warner, W.L. (1937), *A black civilization: a social study of an Australian tribe*, Harper, New York.

Wells, Ann E. (1964), *Stars of Arnhem Land*, Angus and Robertson, Sydney.

Wells, A.E. (1973), *Stars in the sky: legends of Arnhem Land*, 3, Rigby, Adelaide.

White, Isobel M.I. (1975), Sexual conquest and submission in the myths of central Australia in L.R. Hiatt (ed.) *Australian Aboriginal mythology*, Australian Institute of Aboriginal Studies, Canberra.

Willey, Keith (1979), *When the sky fell down: the destruction of the Sydney region 1788–1850s*, Collins, Sydney, London.

Worms, Ernest Alfred (1986), *Australian Aboriginal religions*, Spectrum Publications, Richmond (first published 1968).